IT'S THE REAL THING

SOVIET & POST-SOVIET SOTS ART & AMERICAN POP ART

Regina Khidekel

I0805857

Frederick R. Weisman Art Museum
UNIVERSITY OF MINNESOTA

Distributed by the University of Minnesota Press
Minneapolis London

front cover
Vitaly Komar and Alexander Melamid
Lenin Hails a Cab [detail]

inside front cover
Alexander Kosolapov
Coca-Cola

back cover
Alexander Kosolapov
Malevich Sold Here

This book has been published in conjunction with the exhibition *It's the Real Thing: Soviet and Post-Soviet Sots Art and American Pop Art*, which was organized by the Frederick R. Weisman Art Museum and shown from December 19, 1998, through March 7, 1999.

©1998 Frederick R. Weisman Art Museum.
All rights reserved.

Distributed by the University of Minnesota Press, 111 Third Avenue South, Suite 290, Minneapolis MN, 55401.
http://www.upress.umn.edu

Cover and book design by Jeanne Lee
Printing by Bolger Publications

No portion of this book may be reproduced in any form or by any means without the permission of the copyright holder. For more information, please contact the Frederick R. Weisman Art Museum, 333 East River Road, Minneapolis MN, 55455.

Image on page 71 copyright ©1998 By The Metropolitan Museum of Art.

Khidekel, Regina.
It's the real thing: Soviet and post-Soviet sots art and American pop art /
Regina Khidekel.
Exhibition catalog.
ISBN 0-8166-3445-9
1. Sots art—Exhibitions. 2. Dissident art—Soviet Union—Exhibitions. 3. Pop art—United States—Influence—Exhibitions.
4. Avant-garde (Aesthetics)—Soviet Union—History—20th century—Exhibitions. I. Title.
N6988.5.S67K55 1998
709'.47'074776579—dc21

98-49803 CIP

CONTENTS

acknowledgments

from the director

SOTS ART was a wonderful revelation to the Weisman Art Museum. We were introduced to it by Regina Khidekel, whom we had the pleasure of meeting even before she came to New York from St. Petersburg with her husband, Mark, and their son. Regina was an active part of the life of contemporary art when she lived in Russia and has continued to support Russian artists and to help expose their work to the American audience.

This book documents an exhibition by the same name at the Weisman Art Museum at the University of Minnesota from December 19, 1998, to March 7, 1999. I first want to acknowledge those who contributed to the exhibition itself.

We are grateful, first, to Regina for bringing the idea of this exhibition to us, and for working with us as a guest curator. The unfamiliarity of the material to our staff, and the distance between New York and Minneapolis, did not make the process easier, but Regina's knowledge and unflagging patience and goodwill made up for any difficulties. We worked together in a wonderful partnership to create the exhibition and book. Our staff learned so much from Regina, and from our collaborative process.

First thanks, of course, from both Regina and me, must go to the artists and the lenders for the exhibition. Each lender is listed and we are so grateful for their generosity. The private collectors showed incredible support and concern for the artists through their willingness to lend to the exhibition so that the work of these artists could become better known in this country. A number of collectors offered to lend additional works if we needed them. The artist lenders, also, were generous with their works and their time. Their enthusiasm and cooperation provided the backbone for the project. And, we thank institutional lenders: the Metropolitan Museum of Art in New York, The Tsaritsino Museum in Moscow, and the Jane Voorhees Zimmerli Art Museum, Rutgers, The State University of New Jersey.

Regina and I would also like to thank, especially, Mina Litinsky of the Sloane Gallery of Art for her special help and concern. The Ministry of Culture of Russia also provided information and support.

I want to personally thank all the staff of the Weisman Art Museum, particularly my assistant, Gwen Sutter, who shouldered much of the organizational burden for both the exhibit and this book. She is my right arm, my eyes and ears, proofreader, organizer, and much more—and all at the same time!

Karen Duncan, our registrar, spent much time and effort above and beyond her normal duties for exhibition organization. Museum intern Craig Charles selected the American pop art pieces that are included and did many, many other things. I only hope that his learning experience was as valuable to him as the work he did for this show was to the Museum! Mark Kramer, our installation designer, worked with artists and curators, as usual, to make the show both stunning visually and true to its intellectual and educational goals. All the staff of the Weisman, who are listed elsewhere in this book, deserve an extra special thanks.

For the book, I want to thank our designer, Jeanne Lee, who made this book beautiful and in spite of our best efforts in the other direction, made sure it was produced in time for the exhibit opening. Doug Armato, director of the University of Minnesota Press, provided early support for our concept, and we are pleased that the press will distribute the book. I also want to thank my husband, Blaine, who provided editing for the book—occasionally coerced, but usually cheerfully!

The museum acknowledges and thanks donors to the exhibition, particularly the Hulda and Maurice Rothschild Foundation, Kim and Gloria Anderson, Jennifer Case Phelps, the Carolyn Foundation, Penny and Mike Winton, and Margaret and Angus Wurtele, who made it all possible.

Lyndel King

from the curator

I WISH TO THANK the entire staff of the Frederick R. Weisman Art Museum for their outstanding commitment to make this exhibition a success. I wish especially to thank Lyndel King for her sensitivity and ability to comprehend the idea behind this project and to develop it to its fullest realization. She created a unique atmosphere of intellectual camaraderie and scholarly appreciation that made it a joy to work on this exhibition. *Regina Khidekel*

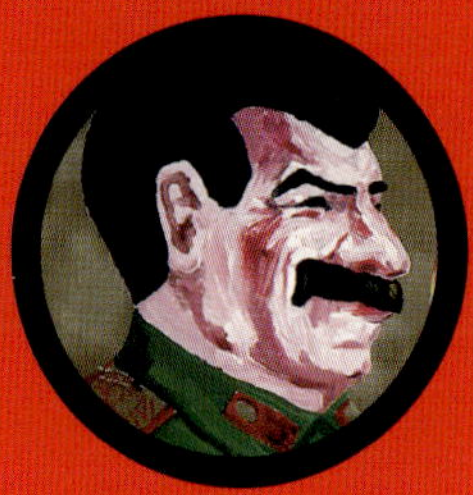

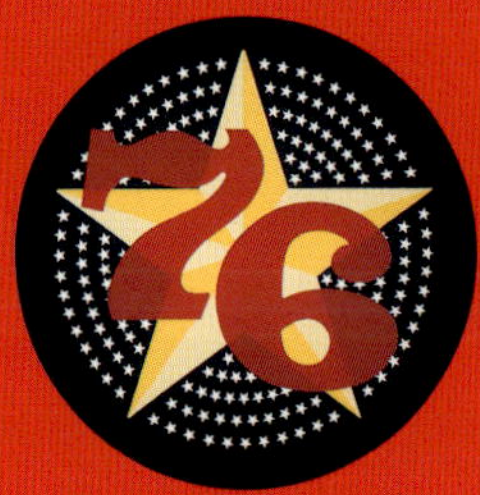

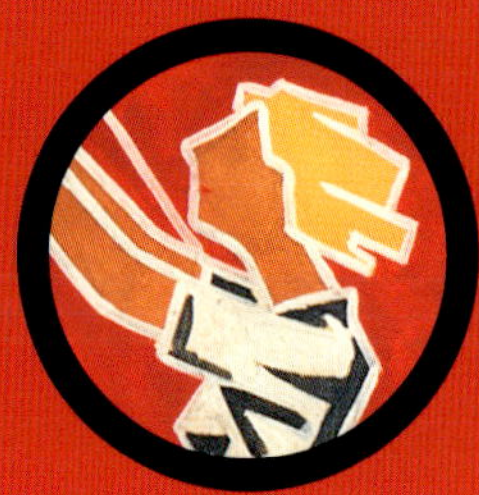

IT'S THE REAL THING

soviet & post-soviet **SOTS ART** & american **POP ART**

Regina Khidekel

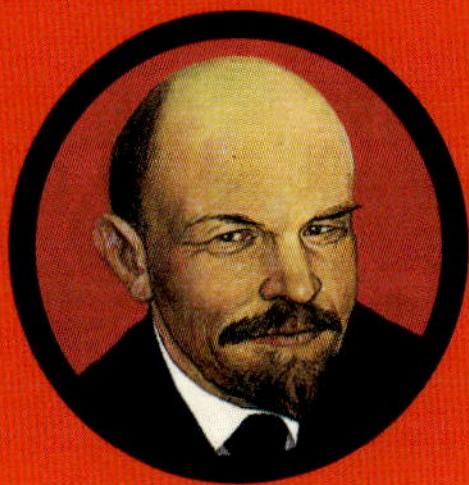
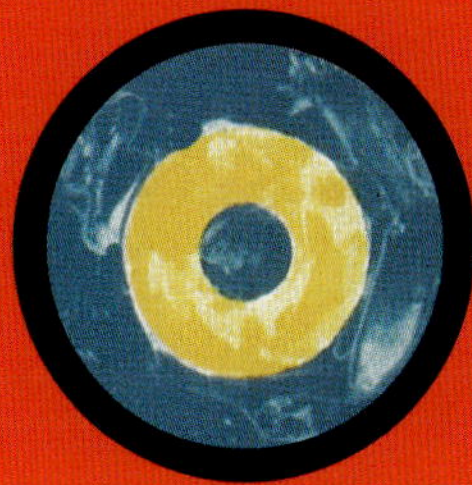
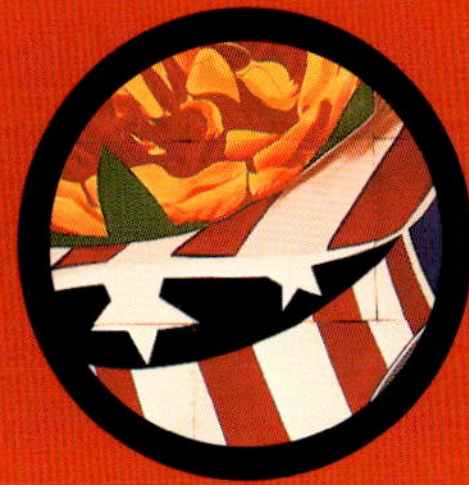

Pop art was invented in America in the 1960s, and sots art, with pop art as its inspiration, came into being in the former Soviet Union during the 1970s. Both expressed and exposed the core elements of their societies: in America, consumerism, and in the USSR, Communist ideology. Pop and sots artists used irony, parody, and mockery as their modus operandi. However, their destinies were different. Pop artists and pop art became part of the mainstream; sots, at least in its first phase, remained underground and marginal and its artists were harassed and misunderstood. Pop and sots, though similar in style and intent, evolved differently because of radical dissimilarities in the political climate and artistic opportunities in America and Russia.

The twentieth century saw the rise of the United States and Russia to the status of superpower. This was a marked shift from the nineteenth century, when both nations had achieved only secondary status in the world of diplomacy and power and maintained scant contact between each other. There were occasional forays by American businessmen seeking opportunity in the tsar's empire, and, of course, there was the sale of Alaska by Russia to the U.S., considered a folly at the time but later regarded as a stroke of American diplomatic savvy.

Since the late nineteenth century the Russian people had seen America as a land of dreams and a place of salvation—a haven against pogroms, religious intolerance, and proscribed social freedoms. At the end of the nineteenth century, millions streamed from Russia to the U.S., but increasingly anti-immigrant sentiment percolated in the United States, giving rise to xenophobic movements that attempted to seal the borders against foreigners, especially to those suspected of political radicalism and "racial inferiority."

With the coming of the 1917 Russian Revolution relations between the nations changed radically. The 1918–1919 antirevolution intervention of the Entente Powers, which included England, France, and the U. S., in the Russian Civil War helped to launch strong and ceaseless anti-American propaganda in the Soviet Union. This campaign continued throughout much of the twentieth century, despite America's generosity in bolstering Soviet industrialization in the 1930s, their World War II alliance, and the Allied effort to send weapons and food to sustain the Soviet Union during its terrible struggle against the Nazis.

Vladimir Galba
costume design for character, "Mister Sam" from A Man from Mars *play (anti-American propaganda)*
1949
gouache, pencil, bronze paint on paper
17 1/8 x 12 1/2 inches
courtesy of Mark and Regina Khidekel

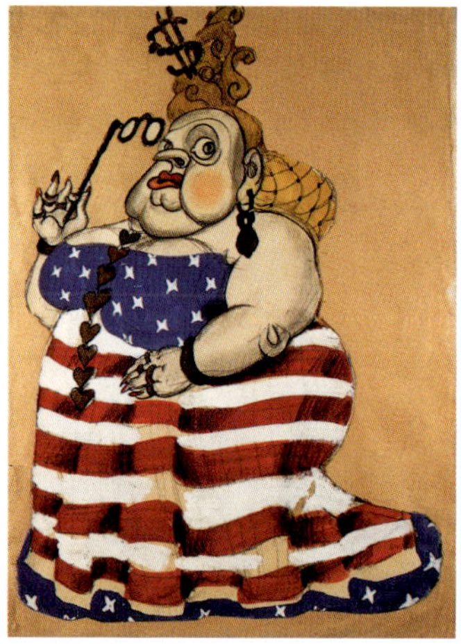

In the post-war atomic era the Soviet Union and the United States became the two acknowledged superpowers and focused all of their hostility and rivalry upon each other. This created a kind of Manichean world of opposites, with the children of light arrayed against the children of darkness. Though their systems of government differed, they were similar in size, power, and influence.

The 1950s McCarthyite hysteria in the United States took the form of the "Red scare"—an often anti-Semitically tainted witch hunt for members of the Communist Party who were supposedly plotting to take over the United States. It targeted mostly intellectuals: writers, actors, and artists. This coincided with the USSR's own "cosmopolitanism" campaign against the intelligentsia that peaked with the anti-Semitic paranoia of the late Stalin era (late 1940s and early 1950s) and the ominous plan to eliminate Soviet Jews. International tensions rose with the outbreak of the Korean war in 1950, and about a decade later, with the Cuban missile crisis, which brought the world to the nuclear brink.

Cultural reactions to these political events varied considerably on both sides of the Atlantic. Americans, regarding the Soviets as their mortal enemies, began preparing for Armageddon by digging bomb shelters. This paranoia coincided with an explosive "outbreak" of consumerism; the hedonistic worship of rock-and-roll stars, movie celebrities, and broadcast superstars; and the improbable entry of mass culture into the world of highbrow art through the emergence of pop art.

In the Soviet Union, Moscow relentlessly churned out anti-American propaganda during the 1950s, but the Russian people would not buy it entirely. With the coming of the thaw after Stalin's death in 1953, millions flocked to foreign movies, exhibitions and festivals, and met foreigners for the first time in decades.

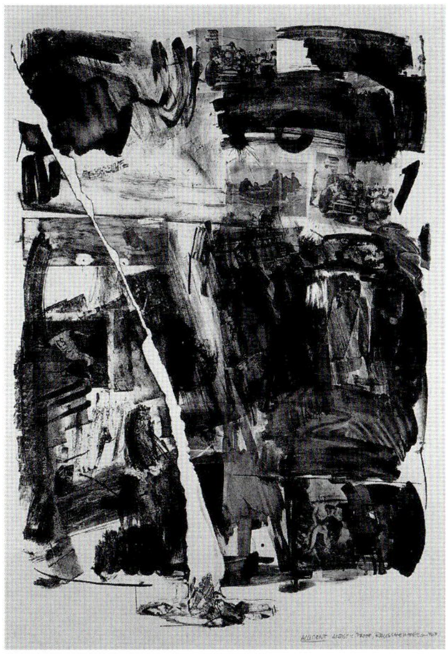

Robert Rauschenberg
Accident
1963
lithograph on paper
41 x 29 1/4 inches
The Minneapolis Institute of Arts

A performance of George Gershwin's *Rhapsody in Blue* in Moscow's Column Hall in 1954 opened a new age. Contemporary American visual art was seen openly in the Soviet Union for the first time in the summer of 1957 during the All World Festival of Youth (July 28–August 11), which presented 4,500 works of contemporary foreign artists from 52 countries. This was the first time the Russian capital saw works by Americans Jackson Pollock and Robert Rauschenberg. During this period several international workshops in Moscow's Central Park of Culture brought together young foreign artists and the curious public, which of course included artists. In January 1957 the magazine *America* was published again in the Soviet Union after a long hiatus. Snappy, glossy, and colorful, it differed radically from the dull and colorless Soviet magazines, and served as a source of information about American popular culture and contemporary art.

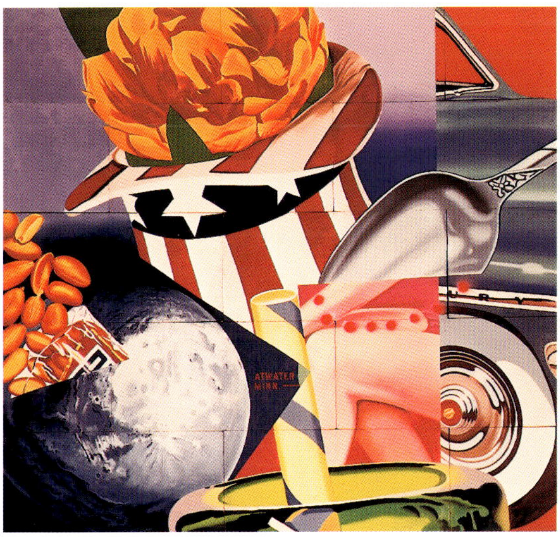

James Rosenquist
World's Fair Mural
1964
oil on masonite
240 x 240 inches
collection of The Frederick R. Weisman Art Museum
gift of the artist

During the late fifties a segment of Russian youth known as *styliag* became fascinated with such products of American mass culture as Coca-Cola, chewing gum, and rock and roll. Fashionable Soviet youth wore high big-heeled boots and hair styles à la Elvis Presley. They chose loud music and dance with a distinctively American look and rhythm—an appropriation that was often superficial but nevertheless indicative of the attempt to break out of the prison of isolation and to assimilate the Western lifestyle and the American image.

This slight thaw also allowed a younger generation of artists, poets, and moviemakers limited possibilities to criticize the Communist system. Among the brightest critical contributions of the period was Elem Klimov's 1964 movie, *Welcome* or *Entrance is Forbidden for Strangers,* which was a direct precursor of the artistic reworking and manipulation of propaganda images that occurred later in sots art. Klimov played with the ambiguity of such slogans as "Children are the Masters of the Camp," parodying Soviet propagandistic posters and using white plaster sculptures to represent such generic figures as the girl-pioneer and boy-sportsman that would be developed and transformed by sots artists.

In 1962, at an art exhibition in Moscow, Nikita Khrushchev expressed his outrage at "modernist deviations" in art in the USSR. The iron curtain, which had become remarkably porous after Stalin's death, fell again with a deadening thud and a chilling effect on artists and intellectuals. Art was, in effect, divided into two parts: official and non-official. This division lasted until the fall of the communist regime in the late 1980s.

Official art was sponsored by the government through the Union of Artists. Dubbed "socialist realism," it was to depict life as it ought to be, namely, perfect. Perfection would be achieved, according to official ideology, by the proper implementation of Communist "theology." Socialist realism was defined not only by its subjects—historical or contemporary scenes that supported Communist goals—but also by its style, a sort of fuzzy realism.

Non-official, or nonconformist, art embraced more stylistic diversity. During the 1960s nonconformist art was oriented toward modernism. It embraced the style of late-nineteenth-century French artist Paul Cezanne, for example, but it was particularly grounded in the spare, geometric forms of Russian art of the first decades of this century, when the avant-garde was abstract and when avant-garde art had been considered appropriate to the new ideas of the Russian revolution. By the time of sots art, in the 1970s, nonconformist artists had experimented with surrealism, and the forms of non-official art were no longer so uniform—or so abstract.

To Soviet artists eager for new forms and new ideas, pop art offered both new forms and new ideas. It provided artists a new way to be avant-garde that was totally different from the spare geometric forms of Russian art from the early decades of this century. Pop art also redirected attention to the outside world and away from the psyche of the painter, which had been at the core of the abstract expressionism of artists such as Jackson Pollock, who had dominated American art at mid-century. The artist was no longer focused on discovering self, but on discovering the world.

James Rosenquist
Spaghetti and Grass
1965
lithograph on paper
31 1/2 x 23 inches
Ione and Hudson Walker
Acquisition Fund
The Frederick R. Weisman Art Museum

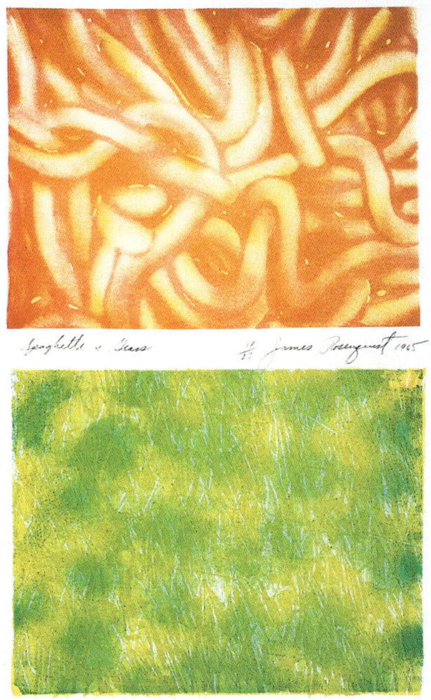

Socialist realism also focused on the world outside—on familiar scenes and objects—but pop art, though its forms were easily identifiable and representational, was resoundingly unlike the realism of official Soviet art. Pop art was iconoclastic. It approached mass culture and familiar objects with irony and the pretensions of the official art world with humor that bordered on mockery. Pop art turned the art world upside down and inside out.

Claes Oldenburg's giant sculptures of such everyday objects as electrical plugs, French fries, and typewriter erasers proclaimed impersonality as a style and transformed the commonplace into art. George Segal took his lifelike and life-sized white plaster figures out of paintings into real environments. Roy Lichtenstein's enlargement of vulgar commercial images from comic

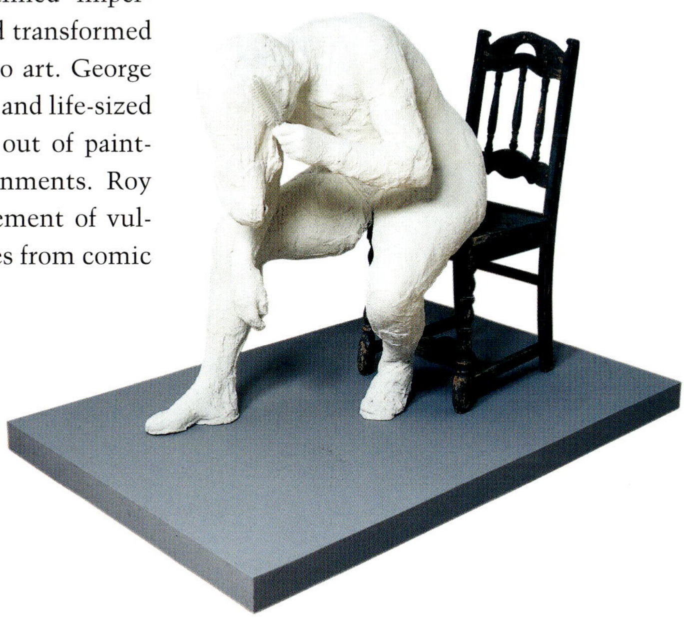

George Segal
Woman Brushing Her Hair on Green Chair
1964
plaster, chair and brush
40 x 43 x 28 inches
collection of Julie and Babe Davis

Roy Lichtenstein
World's Fair Mural [detail]
1964
oil on plywood
240 x 142 inches
The Frederick R. Weisman Art Museum
gift of the artist

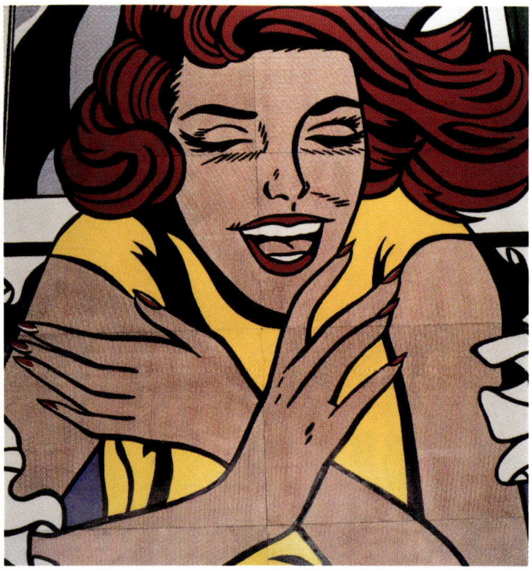

books and advertisements turned comics into art and art into comics. And, Andy Warhol's multiple reproductions and prefabricated images gave pop art a distinctly American finish—cool, commercial, consumerist, and successful. Warhol's notions of equality were based on leveling ideas of democratic consumerism. Everybody drinks Coca-Cola and eats Campbell's soup. Everybody, he proclaimed, would have his "fifteen minutes of fame." In Warhol's pop art world, glamour, style, and fashion were the badge of the artist, not suffering and struggle.

Pop art widened the borders of the avant-garde but simultaneously destroyed the supremacy of form. During the first half of the twentieth century, to be modern and avant-garde had meant to concentrate on pure form. Pop art focused its attention on the profane world of advertising and marketing. Pop art appealed to people through its seemingly optimistic, easy comprehensibility. Indeed, it changed the face of the American art market, bringing to the fore a new generation of collectors, hitherto unaffiliated with the fine arts.

After the division between official and non-official art in the Soviet Union, the artist's choice of an aesthetic became a political issue, a kind of moral resistance. The pervasive lack of information from outside the country forced artists to develop risky relationships with Western diplomats, journalists, and merchants who smuggled in art magazines and books. Since foreigners were allowed, for the most part, only in Moscow, nonconformist artists in the capital were closer to the sources of information and were more aware of the cutting edge of Western contemporary art than their counterparts in Leningrad, which had, in pre-Soviet days, been the place considered more sophisticated and open to influences from the West.

Sots art emerged in Moscow with the second generation of non-official Soviet artists, in the beginning of the 1970s, when pop art had passed its prime in the United States. Sots artists had grown up in the 1960s, the epoch Anna Akhmatova, a great Russian poet of the twentieth century, termed "vegetarian" in contrast with the "carnivore" time of Stalinism.

This generation still remembered the halo of sanctity that surrounded Stalin as the father of the nation and Lenin as its grandfather. Artists of this generation knew how it was to live in a closed society and to embrace absurdity as reality. The first generation of non-official or nonconformist artists rejected the banality of the images that surrounded them and guarded the forbidden modernist aesthetic of abstraction as a spiritual resistance to a repressive society. This new generation was willing to work directly with childhood recollection and the political reality of their own lives. For Russians, politics was their consumerism—the only game in town. Not surprisingly, this younger generation found pop art so appealing because it provided them with the tools to examine the contradictions of their own world and confront the objects of their consumerism—political slogans and official images.

Sots art initiators Vitaly Komar and Alexander Melamid graduated in 1967 from the Stroganov Institute of Design in Moscow. Initially, they collaborated sporadically but from 1972 on they co-signed their works. Energetic, witty, provocative, and playful, they wore many hats —that of artist, critic, and curator. Their manipulation of political subjects was provoked by the prosaic situation of their lives. Komar and Melamid, like other Soviet artists, often made their livings by creating widely distributed propagandistic art for public spaces such as club buildings on collective farms, nurseries, and schools. In the winter of 1972 they worked at a camp for members of the Soviet youth organization Young Pioneers, in a suburb on the Avenue of Cosmonauts, right outside Moscow. While preparing slogans and posters for upcoming activities in their usual playful manner, they became preoccupied by the idea of how to transform this routine work into meaningful, soul-enchanting art.

When told by the camp director of a huge concrete bust of Stalin buried on the grounds, Komar and Melamid found themselves engulfed by a stream of childhood memories of the Stalin epoch, long buried in their unconscious. At first they painted separately in a "propaganda" style—*Portrait of Komar's Wife and Child*, *Portrait of Melamid's Wife*, *Portrait of the Father* and later, *Double Self Portrait*, which depicted their profiles as if on coins—as Lenin and Stalin had been depicted in mosaics in the Moscow subway. They blended the extreme intimacy of family portraits with the dry official stamp of propaganda, ironically highlighting the incompatibility between the objects and the meaning.

Jasper Johns
Target
1974
lithograph on paper
16 x 16 inches
The Minneapolis Institute of Arts

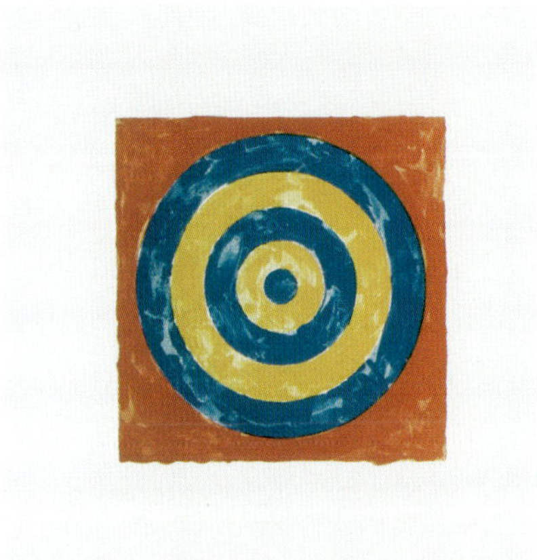

Roy Lichtenstein
Bratatat
1962
pencil and frottage on paper
20 1/2 x 16 1/4 inches
The Minneapolis Institute of Arts

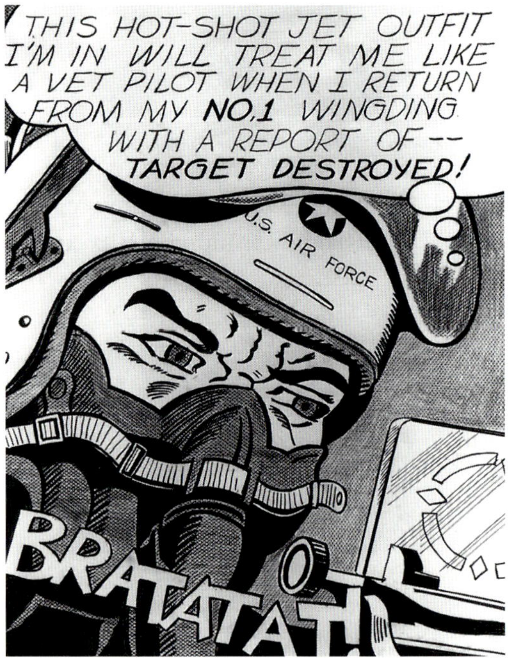

Komar and Melamid also created a parody of the often-depicted slogan "Our Goal is Communism," signing it as if it were their own art work. They came to understand that propaganda art was as much their legacy—and the legacy of Russian art—as the icons of the Russian Orthodox church or the paintings of early-twentieth-century Russian avant-garde movements such as suprematism.

Russian intelligentsia had always had a fondness for theater because it provided a forum, often in a cabaret-like style, for the critical and the satiric. This was especially important during the period when freedom of expression was limited. Komar and Melamid took this tradition of satiric theater to the nth degree, transforming the joke into an artistic trend with consequences they themselves did not at first fully realize.

Komar and Melamid may also have been influenced by Mikhail Bakhtin, a sociologist whose book about medieval folk culture was published in the mid 1960s. Bakhtin's writing brought the whole realm of medieval bawdy humor and lowlife carnival traditions into intellectual critical discourse. It helped smash long-held taboos, such as showing disrespect for authority, and permitted the use of lewd subjects, which had never before figured in Russian art.

Along with their ironic manipulation of ideological images, Komar and Melamid had a special feel for language. They created their own artistic name—"Famous Artists"—as an ironic sign of official recognition and made a mockery of the mythology of "high art" by conceptualist projects such as fictional "well-documented" biographies of artists they invented. One of their inventions was Apelles Ziablov, who supposedly lived in the eighteenth century and whom they termed "the first abstract artist in the world." In keeping with standards for a proper avant-garde artist, Ziablov suffered and finally committed suicide. Another fictional character was Nikolai Buchumov, a strict realist who lost an eye and thereafter always "showed the right side of his nose on the left side of his canvas."[1] Buchumov's supposed precision earned him the title of "supreme realist in the history of art." Komar and Melamid's inventiveness reached such an extreme point that they manufactured a new joint identity and thus abolished their individuality, creating a new artistic collective.

Komar and Melamid created the term "sots" art—an amalgam of socialist realism and pop art. Soviet socialist realism was defined as socialist by content and realism by form. Pop art's forms were realistic, too, but its content was consumerism and mass production. Sots art's realism would define and reinterpret socialist ideology—comparable because ideology was mass produced for "consumers" in the Soviet Union.

The core group of sots artists comprised mostly artists who had graduated in the late 1960s from Moscow's Stroganov Institute of Design, at about the same time as Komar and Melamid. They were, in addition to Komar and Melamid, Alexander Kosolapov, Leonid Sokov, Boris Orlov, artist and poet Dmitry Prigov, and a younger generation of Komar and Melamid's students who formed a group called The Nest, which presented performances from 1975 through 1978.

Alexander Kosolapov, who graduated from the sculpture department of the Stroganov Institute in 1969, began to create pop objects in 1972 and later turned to painting. Between 1972 and 1974 Kosolapov objectified such gestures as that of *The Kefir*—the hand that poured a highly popular and affordable liquid form of buttermilk from the bottle to the glass. This gesture was at once commonplace, reflexive, and ritualistic—ancient as human history and actual in modern life.

Kosolapov was drawn to Andy Warhol, but especially to the contradictions inherent in Claes Oldenburg's giant soft sculptures, which mimic real everyday objects but are obviously totally non-functional. The immo-

1. Carter Ratcliff, *Komar & Melamid* (New York: Abbeville Press, 1988), 66–67.

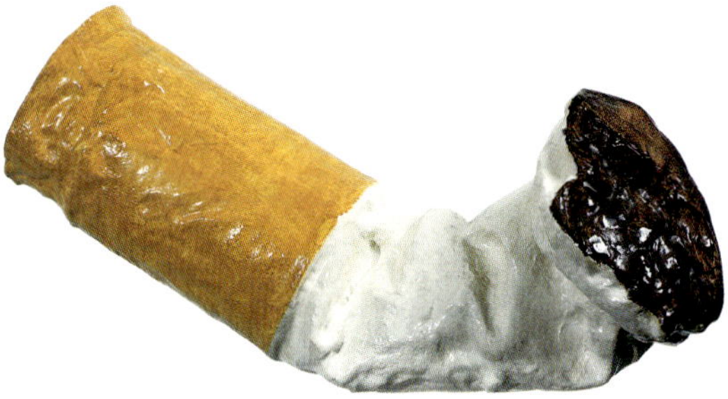

Claes Oldenburg
Cigarette Butt
16 x 10 1/2 x 9 1/4 inches
collection of Miles and Shirley Fiterman

bility of Kosolapov's *A Latch*, constructed from one piece of wood, and the total contradiction of the material and the implied function of his *Crocheted Camera*, make these pieces surrealistic non-functional objects in the Oldenburg tradition. His *Swan Lake* fused high and low culture by combining two very important symbols of Soviet supremacy, the ballerina and the cosmonaut, rendered in a satiric, folklike style. Kosolapov's objects were not exhibited in the Soviet Union.

Leonid Sokov started as an animal sculptor whose work was characterized by folklike grotesquerie. His turn towards pop-sots began in the middle of the 1970s with common objects made in incompatible materials such as a wooden shirt, a ceramic heart, or iron arm. The rough, cracked texture of his wood or ceramic works were made to look primitive, as a reminder of the sloppy, unprofessional finish of Soviet industrial production. His reference to a primitive folk aesthetic and his use of kinetic children's toys allowed him to reveal the utter flatness of mass consciousness through the seemingly harmless device of folk art playfulness.

Ed Ruscha
Double Standard
1969
silkscreen on paper
27 x 40 inches
The Minneapolis Institute of Arts

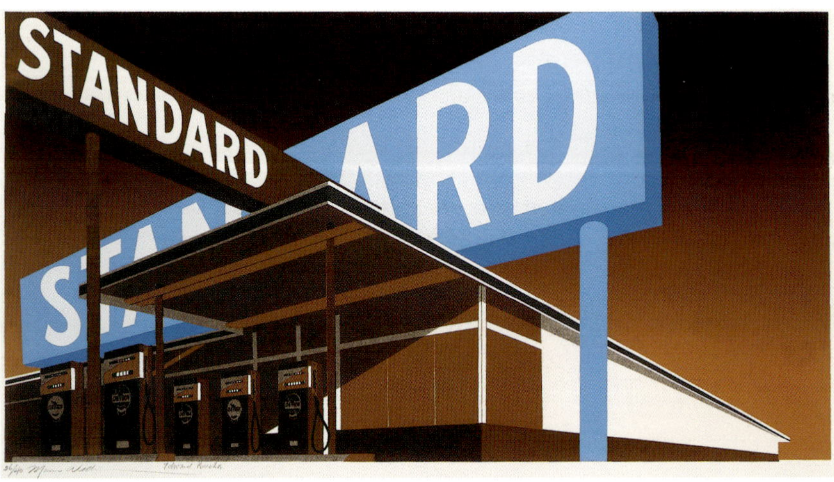

In 1974 Boris Orlov created his first *Emperor*, a model of an imperial monument that had only a facade but nothing more. During the 1980s his favorite hero was a sailor, the most important mythological figure in Soviet history—the very image of its imperial power. Orlov's portraits were totems, a reduction of individuals to beribboned chests groaning under the weight of officialdom. The honors were, however, hollow ones, reminiscent of those awarded to his characters by the nineteenth-century Russian satirical playwright Nikolai Gogol.

Orlov's 1980s objects parodied the military paranoia of the Leonid Brezhnev regime and, particularly, the Afghanistan military "adventure," which began in 1979. Orlov fashioned a creative mix of dynamic portraits with the fanfare of military parades and imperial glamour. His "imperial" style, based on strong compositional structure and an adherence to a strict form and color system, is the essence of an elegance that distinguishes him from the rest of the sots art circle.

The Nest group, which existed from 1975 through 1978, was formed by eighteen-year-old Gennady Donskoy, Mikhail Roshal-Fedorov, and Victor Skersis, all students of Komar and Melamid, whose idea of collective creativity inspired this group. The Nest cultivated an atmosphere of improvisation, playfulness, and joking, as a way of expressing a nihilistic idea toward social, religious, and artistic values. They earned their name "Nest" after a 1975 performance called *Egg Hatching*, during an exhibition of nonconformist art at an unlikely venue, the Permanent Exhibition of Agricultural Achievements in Moscow.

Parody was their main tool. In the 1974 painting *Will Give the Coal Above Plan!* Nest artist Roshal-Fedorov inserted his portrait as the face of a saint in a traditional framed icon with the title slogan as an inscription, replacing the religious message that might normally be found there. Communism as the new religion of the people was the obvious message of this work. The 1978 Nest performances *Race Toward Jerusalem* and *Let's Become One Meter Closer* parodied Soviet policy against Israel and against contacts between Soviet citizens and foreigners.

Other artists who adopted sots ideas later in the 1970s were Rostislav Lebedev and Grisha Bruskin. One of Lebedev's favorite images was of a popular cigarette brand called Kazbek, which included a landscape of the mountainous Caucasus region. Kazbek also was widely known as Stalin's favorite smoke. One of this series appropriated the American Roy Lichtenstein's painting *As I Opened Fire* and combined it with a Kazbek cigarette package cover, making a reference to the unpopular Chechnya war.

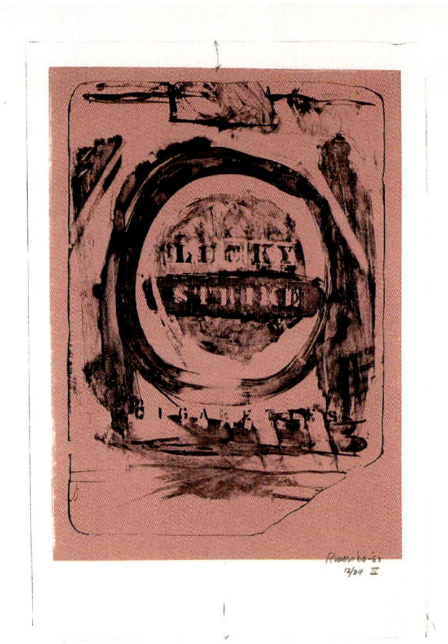

Larry Rivers
Lucky Strike
1964
lithograph on paper
29 1/2 x 20 1/2 inches
The Frederick R. Weisman Art Museum

Grisha Bruskin occupied a special place in the sots art circle because he made his Jewish identity public—a rare and rather dangerous stance at that time. In his visual vocabulary, Soviet mentality and ideology replaced religion's instructive and prohibitive principles. He created a quasi-scientific catalogue of Soviet officialdom classified by profession and social station, which also included references to the Bible and folk mythology. Bruskin was fascinated with the inexpensive white plaster figures that represented different types of Soviet citizens—sportsman, pilot, KGB volunteer, and a soldier with a bordermarker. His work satirized these cheap, garden variety propaganda statues that embodied the didactic "ethics" governing Soviet life.

A major change in sots art occurred in 1978 when its founders Komar and Melamid came to America after having failed to become officially "famous artists" in Soviet Russia. Their participation in the infamous 1974 *Bulldozer Exhibition*, an outdoor exhibition of nonconformist art that was destroyed on the orders of Soviet officials, and their 1976 exhibition in New York at the Ronald Feldman Fine Arts Gallery, were deciding factors for their emigration. By the late 1970s, Alexander Kosolapov, Leonid Sokov, and Vagrich Bakhchanyan were also in New York. In this birthplace of pop art, sots art was recognized as "the first avant-garde movement within the USSR since the 1930s."[2] Sots art entered a new phase during the 1980s when the center of activity moved to New York—it adopted an American look, finish, and size.

For Soviet citizens, including artists, America was swathed in myths of fame and dreams of total freedom. Yet, many Russian émigré artists were not able to crack the American art world. To be sure, there were exceptions, notably the writer Vladimir Nabokov, whose controversial novel,

2. Robert Atkins, *Art Speak* (New York: Abbeville Press, 1997), 151.

Lolita, became notorious in the United States, and the poet Joseph Brodsky, who seemed to understand what made Americans tick.

For Russian émigrés the wave of immigration that started in the 1970s was the first encounter with Western reality. It destroyed many of their illusions and provoked a kind of nostalgia that often accompanies immigration. But contrary to those aristocrats who escaped Communism in 1917, immediately after the Russian Revolution, this later generation of immigrants had nothing to lose except childhood memories and naive expectations about the West. The complicated feelings of this generation of émigrés were ironically interpreted in the works of New York sots artists during the 1980s. Russian artists in the United States had a love-hate relationship with their Soviet past; they felt nostalgic towards it, and yet they were gratified as they realized that its repressive days were numbered.

Komar and Melamid's 1981–82 *Nostalgic Socialist Realism* series was vital in defining the New York phase of sots art. At once subversive and nostalgic, and totally ironic, they used the techniques of high academicism—enormous scale, realistic figures, grandiose subjects, and a highly finished surface—to satirize the representational style of official Soviet art.

Their painting from this series, *The Origin of Social Realism*, presents Stalin and his muse—his inspiration. Though borrowing from the subjects and techniques of the immense academic history paintings of the nineteenth century, it verges on the surrealistic with its gigantic architectural background swathed in symbolic red drapery, evocative of the power of the unconscious and the erotic. Presenting the muse, or pure inspiration, as the source of official painting was an ironic statement about an art that was prescribed and didactic. At the same time, the idea of Stalin in the presence of this muse-goddess captured the repressed but lingering love of many Soviet citizens for Stalin as a

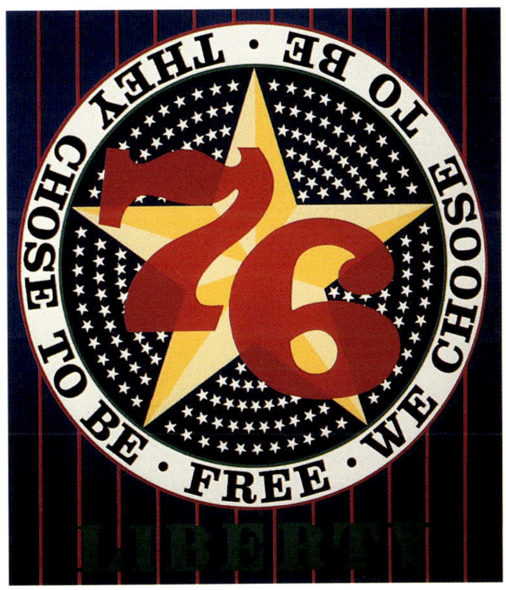

Robert Indiana
Liberty 76
1976
from the Kent Bicentennial Portfolio
screenprint on paper
40 x 36 inches
collection of Walker Art Center, Minneapolis
Art Center Acqusition Fund, 1976

potent leader at the height of his powers of erotic seduction. Themes of death and eroticism symbolized the mystic power of Stalin as cruel patriarch, the so-called father of the nation, and his dark and bloody deeds. Soon Komar and Melamid transplanted their subversive vision to American heroes, creating a series about such sacrosanct national heroes as George Washington, Franklin Roosevelt, and Ronald Reagan.

In the United States Alexander Kosolapov appropriated the consumerist images of pop art and added a Soviet twist, as in *Coca-Cola,* which combined Coca-Cola's world-wide recognizable trademark and slogan, "It's the real thing," and an iconic profile of Lenin. *McLenin, Malevich Sold Here,* and *Thwip* continued this approach. The power of these works lies in their combination of Soviet Communist propagandist images and American advertising images—the propaganda of both societies.

Leonid Sokov retained his folklike (*lubok*) toys of his Soviet days, but added American popular culture celebrities Marilyn Monroe and Elvis Presley to his previous repertoire of Soviet leaders or such traditional Russian symbols as the bear. Sokov loved to pair the sultry glamour of American screen goddesses with lumbering bears or with Stalin himself, as in his 1990 *Lips and Moustaches,* in which Soviet dictator Joseph Stalin and Marilyn Monroe are locked in a crude embrace, framed by multiple images of her famous toothy smile and his bushy black moustache.

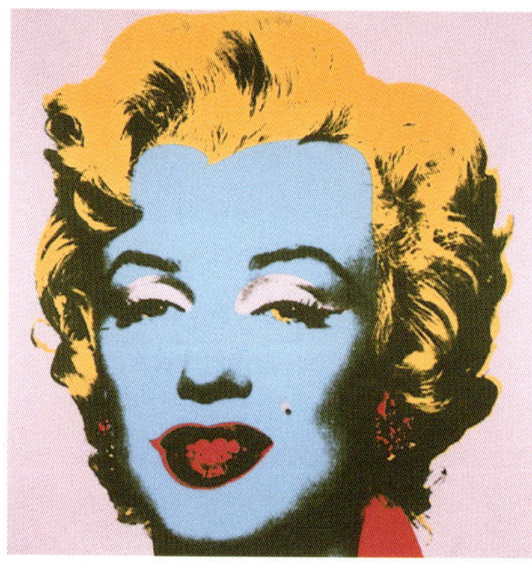

Andy Warhol
Marilyn
1967
serigraph on paper
36 x 36 inches
The Frederick R. Weisman Art Museum
gift of George Shea and Gordon Locksley, by exchange

A new wave of immigration in the 1980s added new ideas to the Komar and Melamid group. Leonid Lamm, who appeared in New York in 1982, added the influence of his training in the Russian avant-garde movements of the early twentieth century and his three-year incarceration in Soviet jails. He was fascinated with American symbols and icons, billboards, and the manufactured look. His 1991 *Untitled* juxtaposed Washington and Lenin, and *Dollar,* from 1990–93, spoofed both America and Russia by combining the Soviet hammer with the American dollar.

The "Kazimir Passion" group, which included Ludmila Bardina, Alexander Drewchin, Victor Tupitsyn, and the American-born Vladimir Urban, settled in New York in the mid 1980s. "Their performances demonstrate one of the important and problematical characteristics of sots art: viewers are never given a chance to figure out whether the artists are seriously propagandizing or only confronting them with an ironic game," wrote curator Margarita Tupitsyn.[3]

With the relatively sudden, final collapse of the Soviet Union in 1991, artists realized they were witnessing an epic-scale event in the history of the world. The rapid changes provoked a certain nostalgia for the lost, absurd world of the Soviet Union and a more pointed criticism of the shallow values of American consumerism that had been at the heart of pop art in the 1960s. Komar and Melamid, by the early 1990s internationally recognized artists, proposed the Monumental Propaganda project in 1992. This proposal sought to alter the destiny of Soviet monuments—many of which had already been destroyed—by offering to change the meaning and purpose of Lenin's Mausoleum by replacing his body with a running tape of advertising messages—surely a pointed comment on the not always positive replacement of one set of insipid ideological slogans with another.

Even after the fall of Communism, ideology continues to be the essential fabric of Russian life. Today, nationalism and Russian culture and religion are the mainstays of the new ideology. It is not surprising that sots art works such as Roshal-Fedorov's *Will Give the Coal Above Plan!*, which satirizes all of these, as well as the Soviet system of industrial production, are no more welcome in post-perestroika Russia than they were in the Soviet Union.

In their use of images of popular culture and politics, the new movements in contemporary Russian art reflect the continuing influence of the sots art point of view. By liberating culture from generations of accumulated fear, by embracing political changes and alternatives, sots artists created a new Russian artistic mentality. They forced open the closed world of the Soviet Union of the 1970s by fusing the most up-to-date in international art movements—pop art—with local ideology. Sots art, the first post World War II Russian art trend recognized in the West as innovative and on a par with other international art movements of the twentieth century, continues to mark contemporary Russian art just as pop art changed the American art world forever.

3. Margarita Tupitsyn, *Sots Art: Russian Mock-Heroic Style* (New York: The Semaphore Gallery, 1984), n.p.

1 EARLY SOTS ART

IN MOSCOW EMBRACES THE DECADE FROM **OSCAR RABIN**'S *PASSPORT* IN 1964 TO THE MID-1970S, WHEN MAJOR SOTS ARTISTS SUCH AS **ALEXANDER KOSOLAPOV**, **VITALY KOMAR**, **ALEXANDER MELAMID**, AND **LEONID SOKOV** WERE COMPELLED TO EMIGRATE BECAUSE OF REPRESSIVE GOVERNMENT POLICIES. THE SMALL SIZE AND ROUGH QUALITY OF THE ART OBJECTS, MADE IN SMALL BASEMENT STUDIOS, DURING THIS FIRST PERIOD OF SOTS ART REFLECT THEIR UNDERGROUND ORIGINS.

Moscow artists Oscar Rabin and **Mikhail Roginsky** may be considered precursors of sots art because they drew their inspiration from the commonplace forms of everyday life. They represented easily identifiable objects that served as recognizable icons of the communal reality of Soviet citizens—a reality that was impoverished and somber in spirit. Rabin was the first to incorporate politically charged objects into his expressionistic paintings and collages. Roginsky's large-scale, flat representations of common objects tied him to pop art in terms of style and content.

IN MOSCOW

Pop art made its way into the Soviet Union via a few sanctioned exhibitions but mainly by the route of smuggled books and magazines. Pop art's legitimization of everyday images inspired artists such as **Ilya Kabakov**, who were part of a movement called "Moscow conceptualism." These artists attempted to interpret the significance of specific Soviet experience that was beyond the purview of what had previously been the accepted form of underground art—the abstract formalism that dominated Western art for most of the first half of the twentieth century. Kabakov created an album format for telling fictional stories of a common Soviet citizen whose mentality was shaped by the forced intimacy of the communal kitchen. He adopted American pop artist Jim Dine's style of representation of common objects to emphasize that in Soviet society, the absurd was accepted as normal.

Vitaly Komar and Alexander Melamid, who coined the term "sots" from pop and Soviet socialist realism, subjected Soviet ideology to the same kind of witty subversion that pop artists did to American consumerism. They exposed Soviet ideology's emptiness and the blind mesmerism of the heroic images of sanctioned Soviet socialist realist art. Their 1972 diptych of the Artists' Wives was part of a series that was the starting point for sots art.

Alexander Kosolapov's 1974 installation and Leonid Sokov's 1976 studio presentation were two significant events of Soviet underground art. They grafted pop ideas, particularly the American Claes Oldenburg's transformation of banal, everyday objects into monumental sculptures, to their world of banal, everyday ideology. Kosolapov's *Aurora* transformed the famous battleship of the 1917 Russian revolution into a romantic sunset on a calm lake. Sokov's use of incompatible materials and scale, and of Russian folk art forms, created subversive, rough images that satirized the Soviet government's pretensions of maintaining a national culture.

In the early 1970s **The Nest group** (**Genady Donskoy**, **Mikhail Roshal-Fedorov**, and **Victor Skersis**) and artists **Eric Bulatov**, **Oleg Vassiliev**, **Boris Orlov**, and **Rostislav Lebedev** focused on Soviet systems for promulgating ideology and creating mythology.

OSCAR RABIN

Passport
1964
oil on canvas
47 1/4 x 35 7/16 inches
courtesy of Natalia Kropivnitskaya

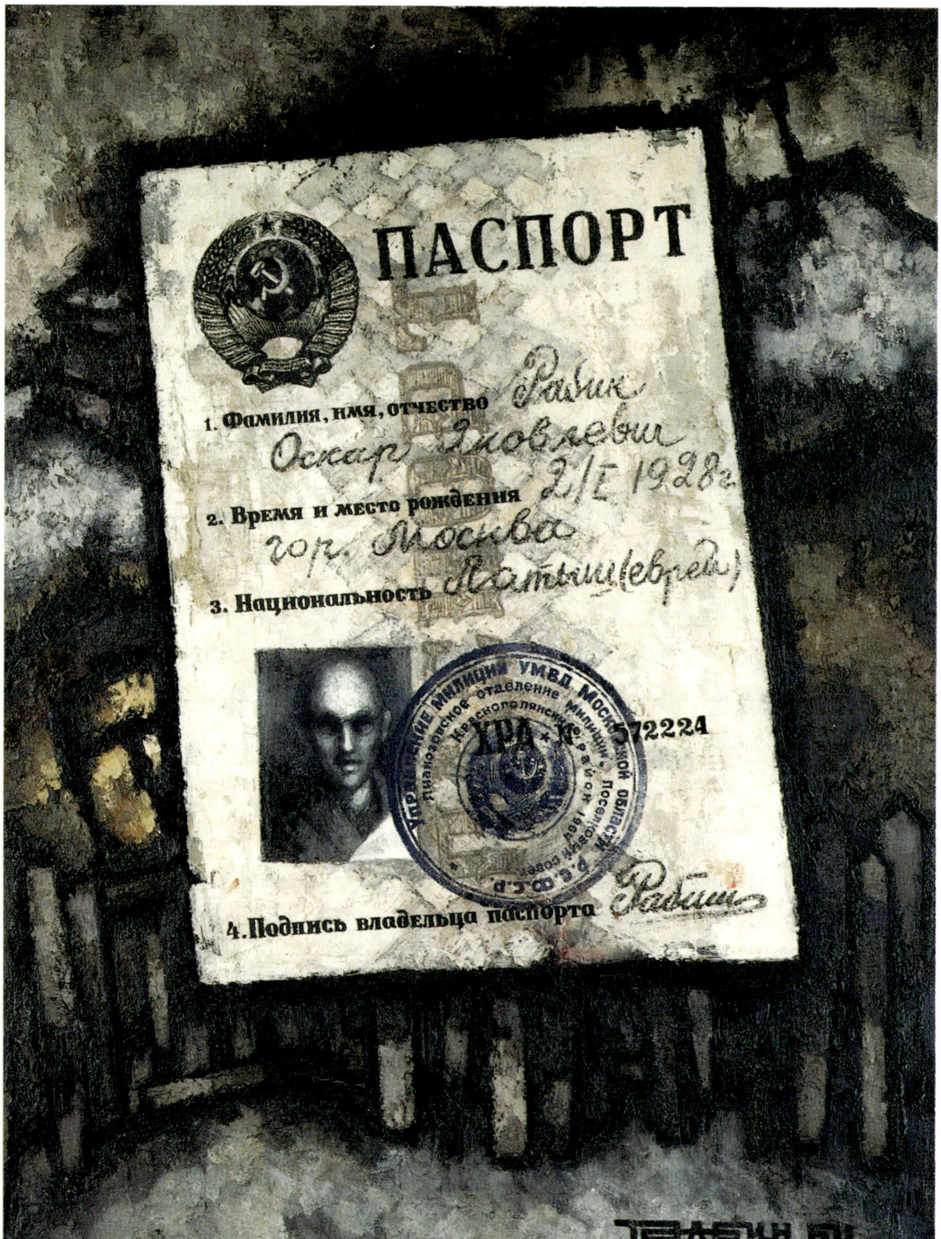

Oscar Rabin was one of the first Moscow artists to incorporate in his paintings such common objects as Bichky cans and vodka bottles to describe the pedestrian life in Moscow's barrack-like suburbs—impoverished, gloomy, and cheerless—where he lived for a long time. His use of a Soviet passport in his painting had a politically charged message in a society where travel was restricted and passports were not automatically issued to any citizen who applied for one. Farmers who lived on collective farms, for example, had no passports because for decades they were restricted from leaving their farms.

A passport also indicated that the holder had the right to live permanently in a particular place, a right that was strictly limited in the cities of Moscow and Leningrad (now St. Petersburg). The Soviet passport was infamous because of its fifth paragraph, which indicated "nationality," and was used to identify—and sometimes persecute—Jews. In this work Rabin represents himself as a Jew and a former citizen of Latvia, a republic that was occupied by the Soviet army in 1939.

MIKHAIL ROGINSKY

Primus Stove 1-2-3
1965
oil on canvas
31 5/8 x 25 3/4 inches
courtesy of the Jane Voorhees Zimmerli Art Museum, Rutgers,
The State University of New Jersey, The Norton and Nancy Dodge Collection of
Nonconformist Art from the Soviet Union

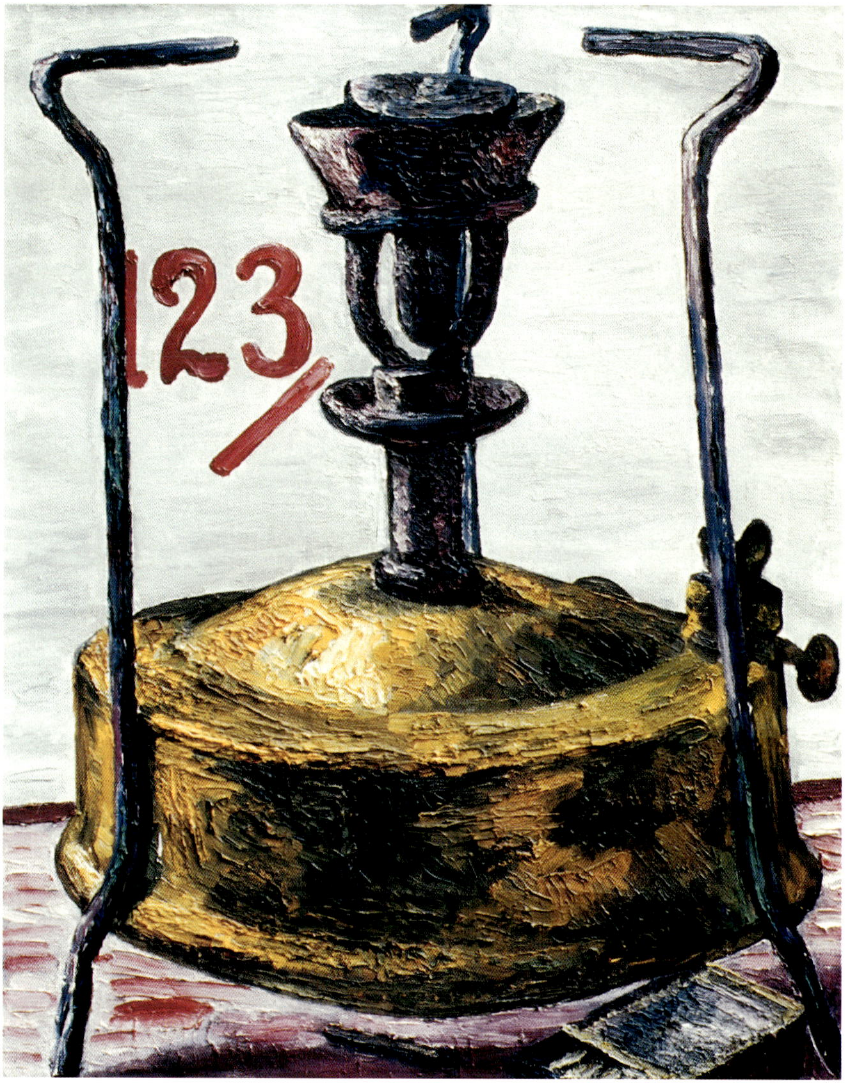

Roginsky, a sots art precursor, used common objects as subjects for his paintings. The Primus stove, a small kerosene stove used for cooking, was the staple of Soviet home life, where communal kitchens and tiny apartments were a grim reality of everyday life. Though the painting is relatively small, Roginsky elevated the status of the stove by filling the whole canvas with its "portrait."

VAGRICH BAKHCHANYAN

Untitled
1969
transfer process, colored pencil
14 x 17 1/2 inches
courtesy of the Jane Voorhees Zimmerli Art Museum, Rutgers,
The State University of New Jersey, The Norton and Nancy Dodge Collection of
Nonconformist Art from the Soviet Union

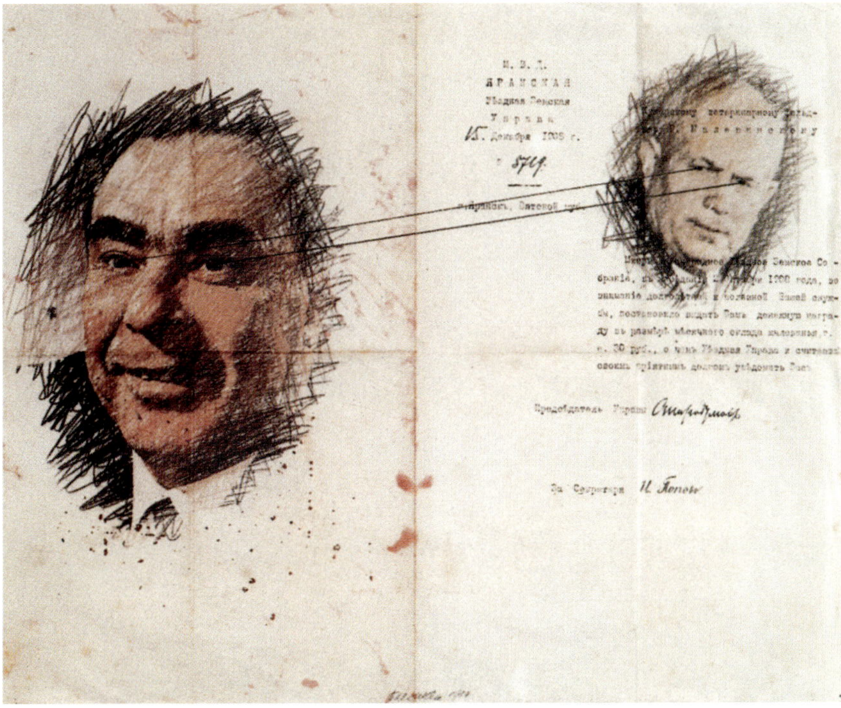

Bakhchanyan manipulated well-known quotes and clichés to create absurd images, often with political meaning. This one represents the portraits of Nikita Khrushchev and Leonid Brezhnev. Khrushchev controlled the Soviet Union from Stalin's death in 1953 until he was ousted in 1964 in a plot masterminded by his successor, Leonid Brezhnev, and others. The two portraits are superimposed on what appears to be a pre-revolutionary decree dated 1909, but the contents of the document refer to a payment by landowners to Khrushchev for a job well done. Khrushchev seems to be glaring at Brezhnev, who has a satisfied smile. Perhaps the work refers to a charge that Brezhnev and his coconspirators used to help oust Khrushchev.

MIKHAIL CHERNISHOV

Squadron (Colonial, German, Russian, French)
1961
collage and watercolor on paper
22 x 22 1/4 inches
courtesy of the artist

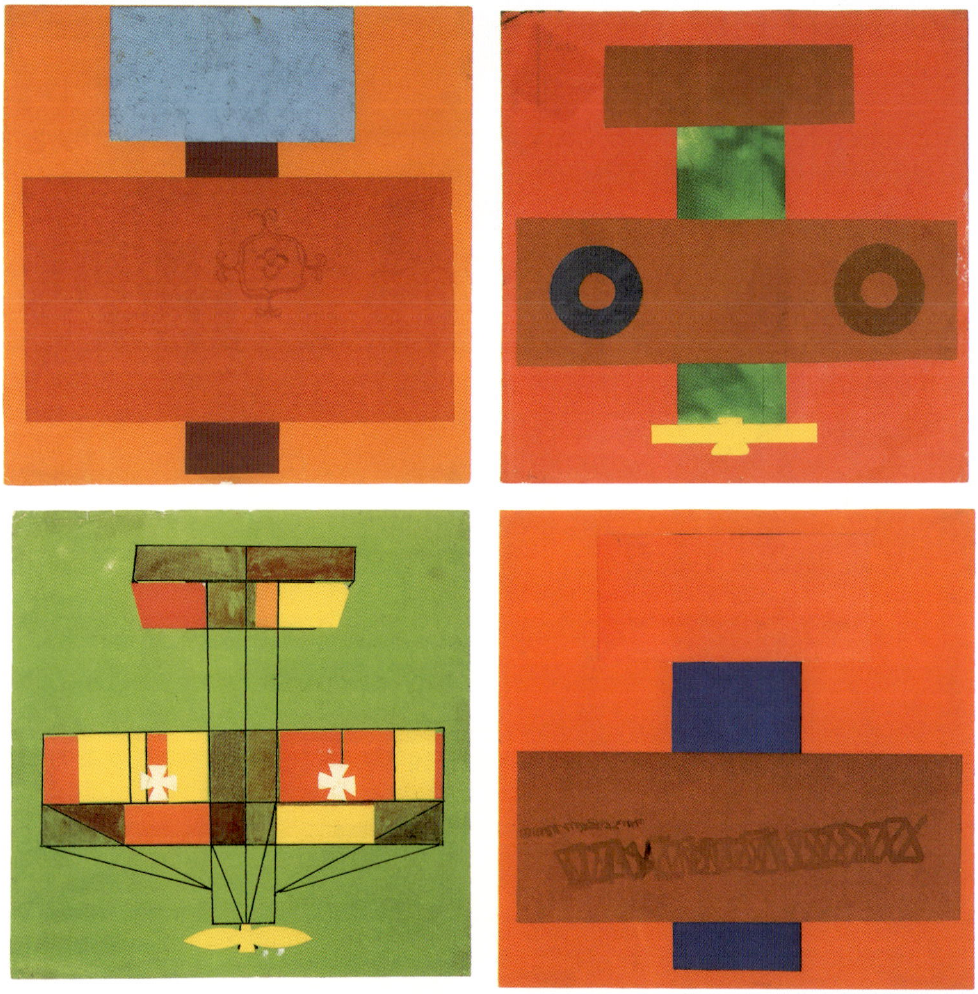

Squadron depicts hostile military planes almost as toys, to sarcastically represent the "Western threat" during a time when the Soviet anti-American propaganda machine was cranked up full force. Even as a teenager, Chernishov was one of the best informed Russian artists about art developments in the West. He was influenced by Roy Lichtenstein, whom he saw in an American art magazine as early as 1962—before the U. S. State Department exhibition of contemporary prints that included American pop art traveled to the Soviet Union in 1963. In some works Chernishov framed pieces of commercial wallpaper to provocatively negate all artistic meaning and form.

MIKHAIL CHERNISHOV

The Round Earth
1963
tempera on paper
18 15/16 x 17 5/8 inches
courtesy of the artist

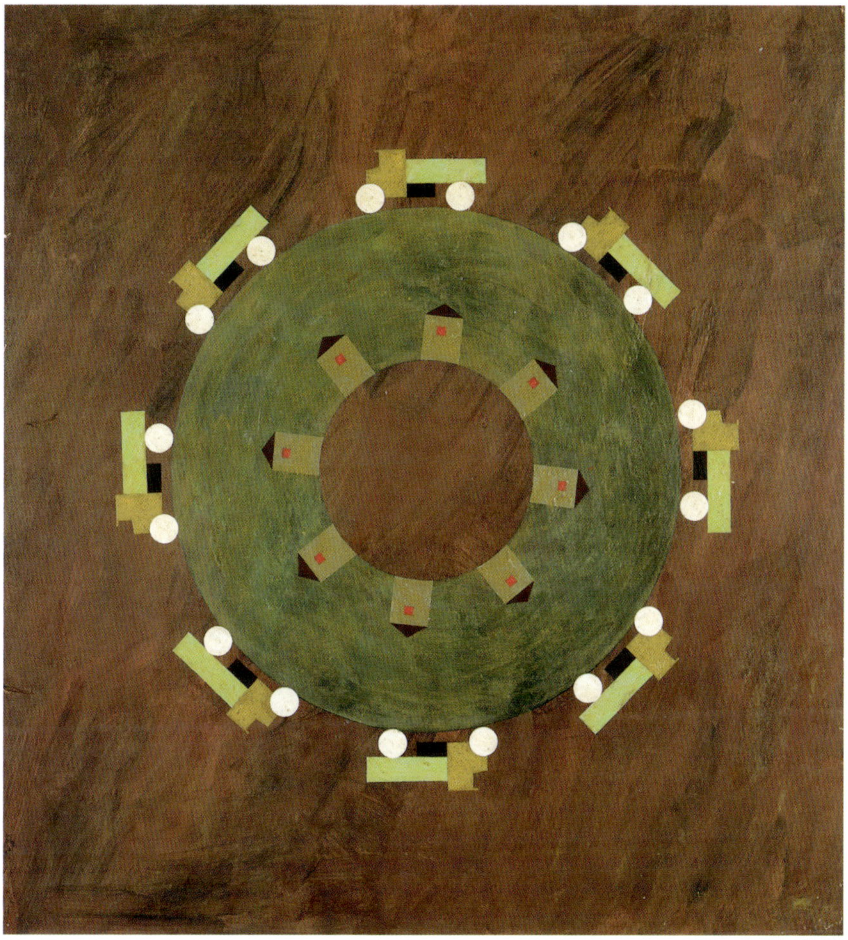

This cheerful geometric, almost child-like, work shows the earth as a disc, populated by identical houses equally spaced around an inner ring and uniform trucks, circling it on the outer edge. It may be a comment on the Communist party goals of standardizing society and dominating the world.

Chernishov sometimes cut pictures of houses, airplanes, and cars out of Soviet magazines and used them in collages, inspired by Moscow subway murals that vulgarized the pure geometry of early-twentieth-century Russian suprematist and constructivist compositions.

ILYA KABAKOV

Small Gallery
1968
colored pencil and ink on paper
12 1/4 x 12 1/4 inches
courtesy of Anatoly Bekkerman, ABA Gallery, New York

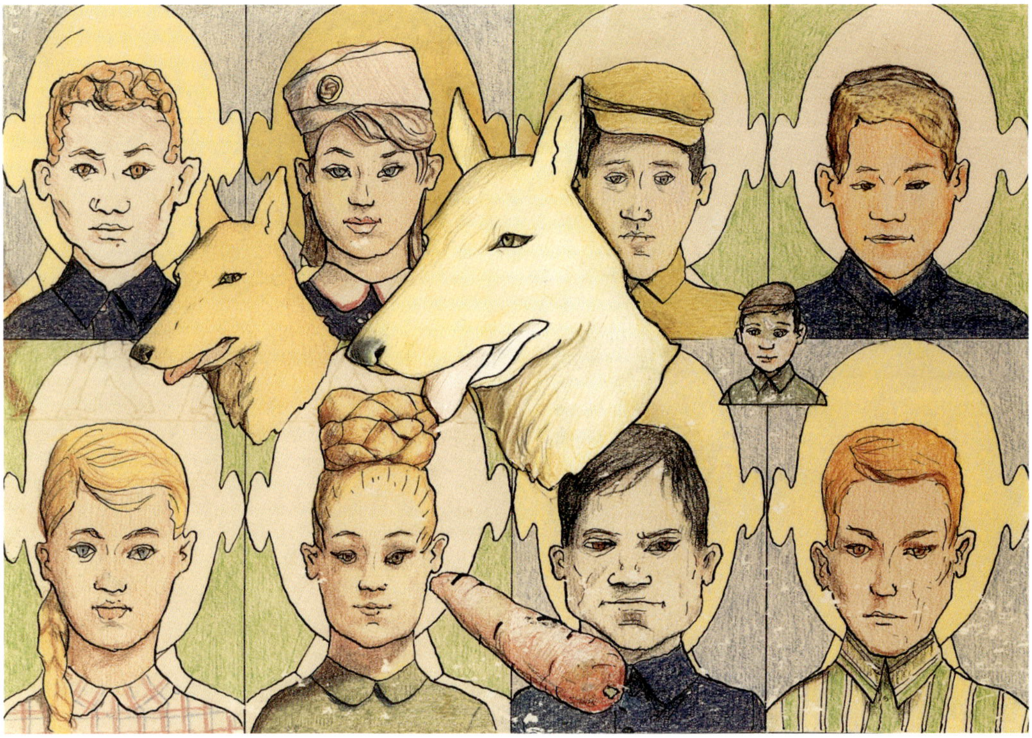

Kabakov worked as a children's book illustrator for some time. His small gallery of children's portraits shows them already in the uniforms of Soviet children's organizations, with identical, anonymous adult heads as shadows behind them to indicate that they all were expected to fit into identical molds as adults. The carrot aimed at the face of one child shows the absurdity of this social system.

LEONID LAMM

Landscape
1959 (book cover design)
gold, enamel, colored marker, colored pencil, masonite, and wood
21 x 14 1/4 x 1 3/8 inches
courtesy of the artist

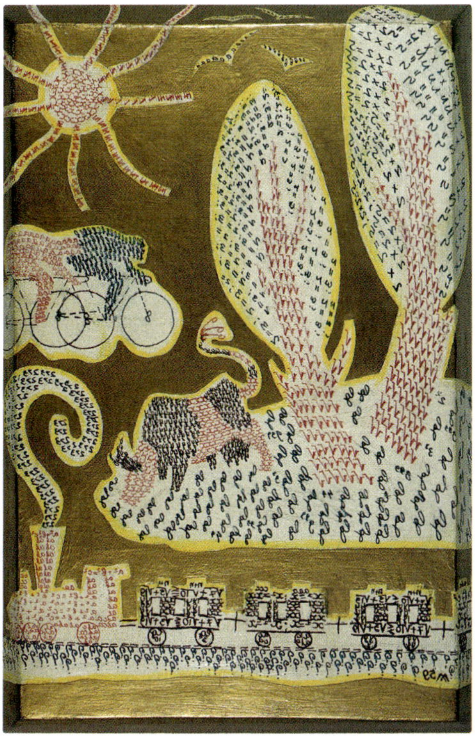

Leonid Lamm, as was the case with many nonconformist artists such as Eric Bulatov, Ilya Kabakov, and Oscar Vassiliev, made his living as a book illustrator. These artists preferred to illustrate children's books because they provided more freedom to use allegories and create fantasies. Also, illustrating children's books allowed them to simplify their images to make them more like the advertising and comic book images of American pop art. In this design, pop art influenced Lamm to represent serious scientific concepts as casual banalities of everyday life.

VITALY KOMAR

Portrait of Komar's Wife and Child
1972
tempera on plywood
25 1/2 x 17 3/4 inches
courtesy of the artist

ALEXANDER MELAMID

Portrait of Melamid's Wife
1973
oil on canvas
25 3/16 x 17 11/16 inches
courtesy of the artist

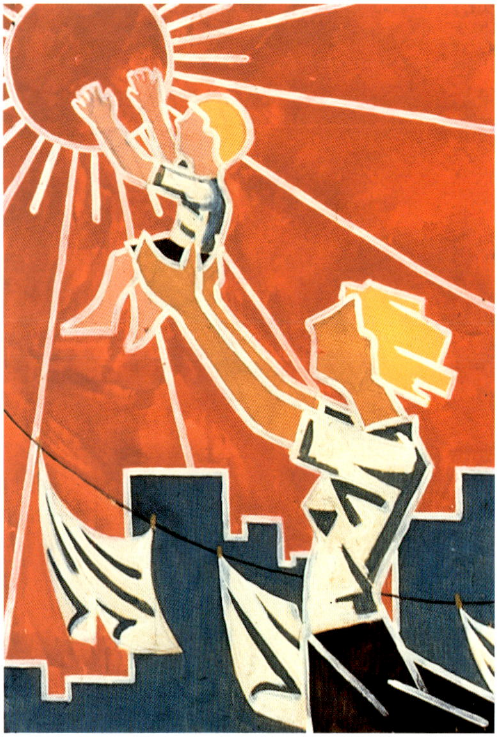

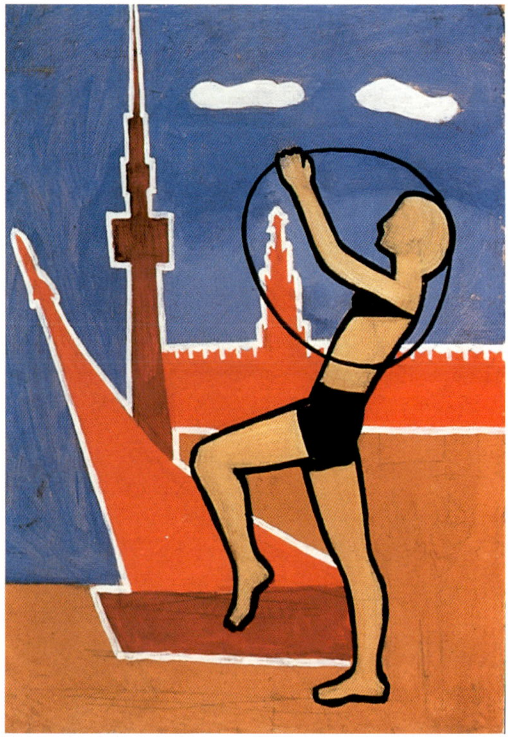

Komar's wife holds up their child who reaches for the sun, a typical subject of Soviet official art, which painted a rosy picture of life under the Soviet system—if not today, then in the future. Strong athletes were the pride of the Soviet system and were often represented in Soviet propaganda art. Melamid's wife is depicted as an athlete with the towers of Moscow in the background. The style of the paintings pokes fun at Soviet propaganda posters.

VITALY KOMAR AND ALEXANDER MELAMID

Five-Year Pig Production Plan
about 1974
oil on canvas
23 1/2 x 29 3/8 inches
courtesy of Alfred and Pie Friendly

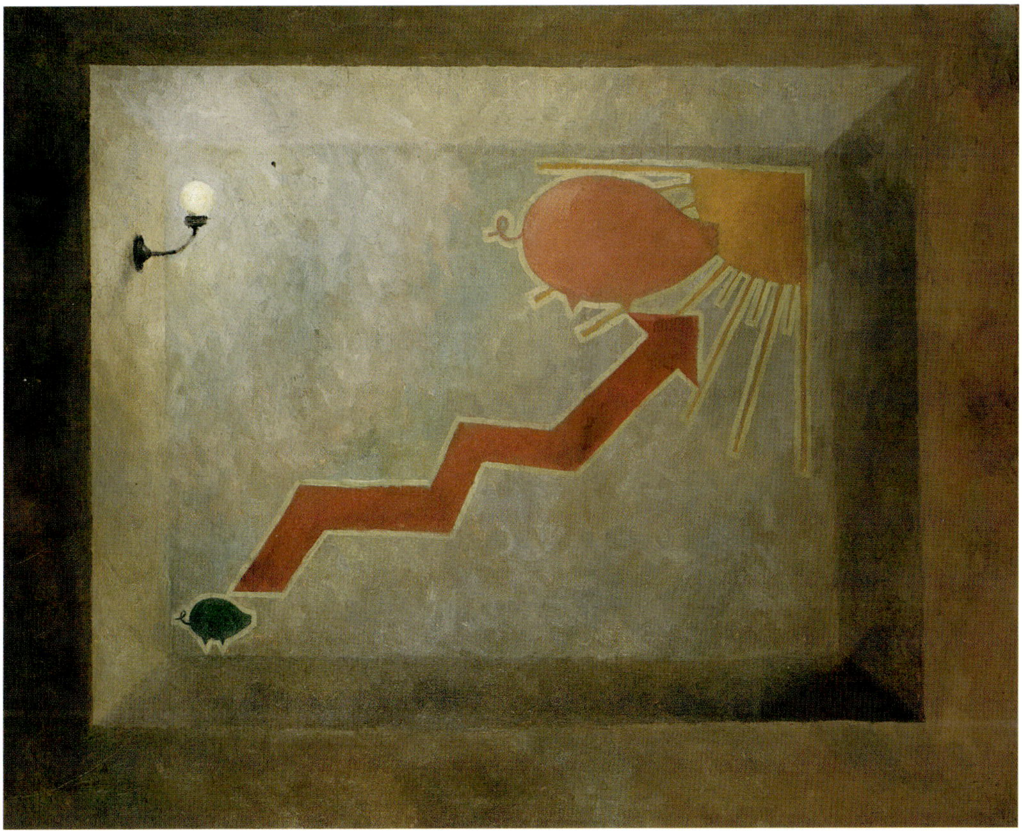

Various five-year plans for industrial and agricultural production were the hallmarks of the Soviet economic system. This painting represents a small blue pig joined by a large red graphlike arrow to a huge pink one that seems to be landing snout first on the sun. The painting's symbolism of the "red" or Communist arrow, which seems to turn the pig into a fat balloon that reaches the sun, mocks these five-year plans, which failed more often than not.

VITALY KOMAR AND ALEXANDER MELAMID

Ahead to the Victory of Communism
1974
oil on fabric
19 3/4 x 75 inches
courtesy of Douglas Davis

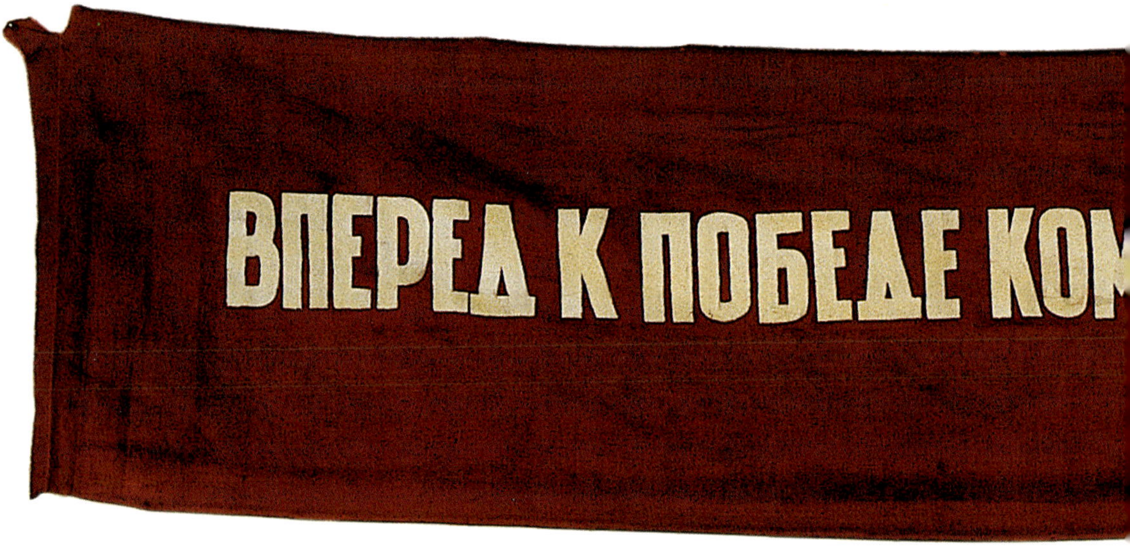

VITALY KOMAR AND ALEXANDER MELAMID

Glory to Labor
1975
oil on fabric
24 x 83 1/2 inches
courtesy of Alfred and Pie Friendly

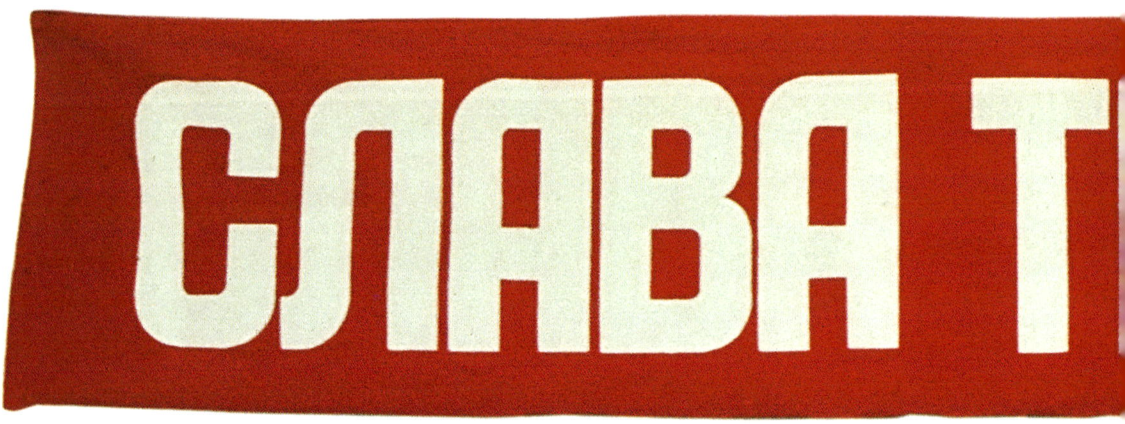

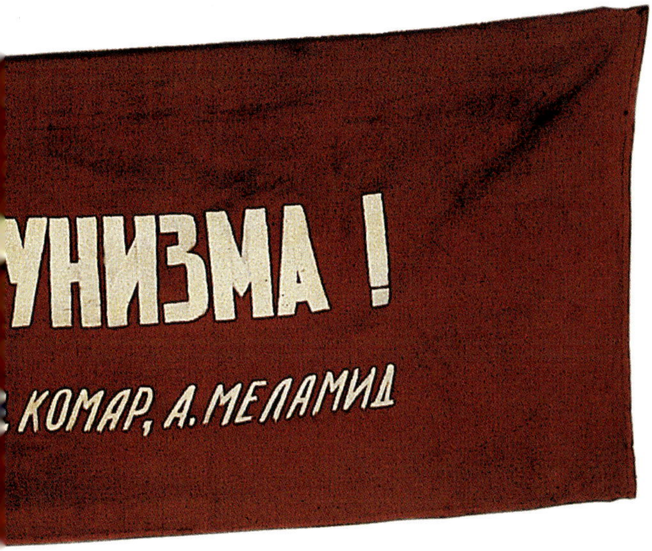

Signing it as their own art work, Komar and Melamid represented familiar propaganda banners as a unique Russian art form. In doing this, they harkened back to the European dada movement of the early twentieth century, which made familiar, mass-produced objects into works of art simply by adding an artist's signature.

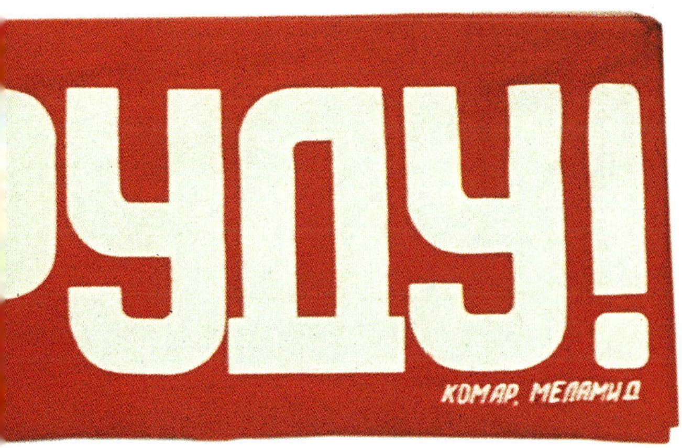

By making these Communist-style slogan banners, familiar to all Soviet citizens, the ironic subjects of their art, Komar and Melamid represented ideological slogans as numbing the minds of the Soviet people in the same way American pop artists represented advertising slogans as having the same effect on Americans.

VITALY KOMAR AND ALEXANDER MELAMID

Article #190.1
1975
oil on canvas
28 3/4 x 19 5/8 inches
courtesy of Alfred and Pie Friendly

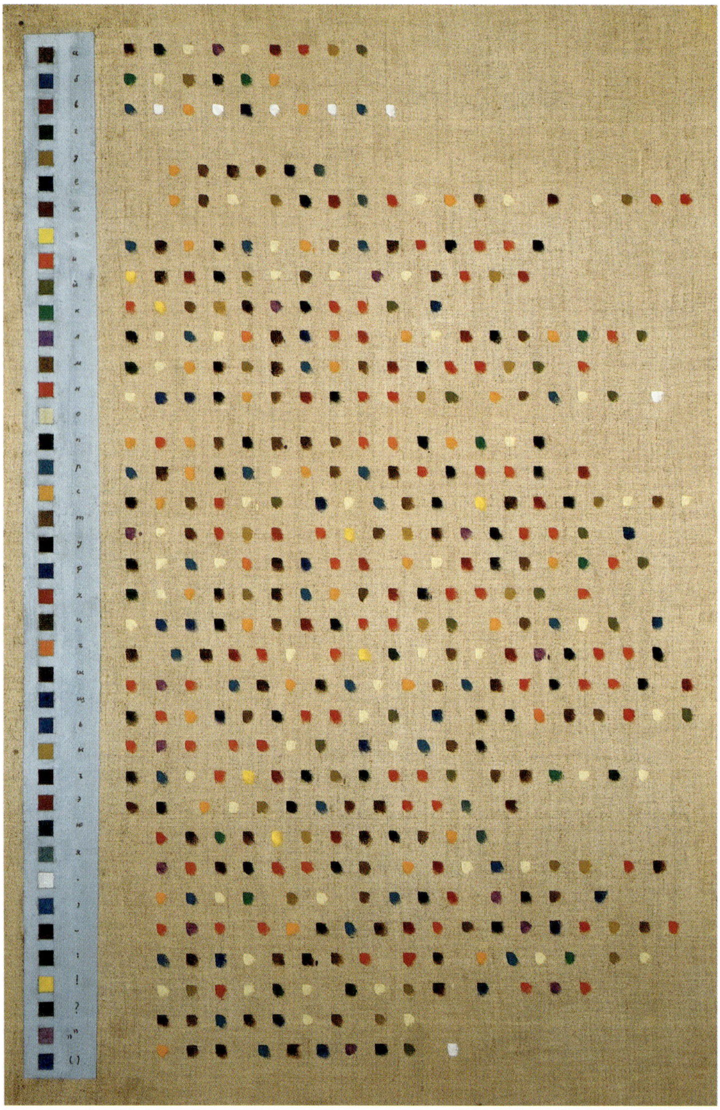

This is part of a series called "Color Writing: Ideological Abstraction." In the Soviet Union, any unauthorized political activities were forbidden. Komar and Melamid created, in this series, a color code to refer to such issues as freedom of speech.

VITALY KOMAR AND ALEXANDER MELAMID

Performance in Paradise
1973
ten photographs
courtesy of the artists

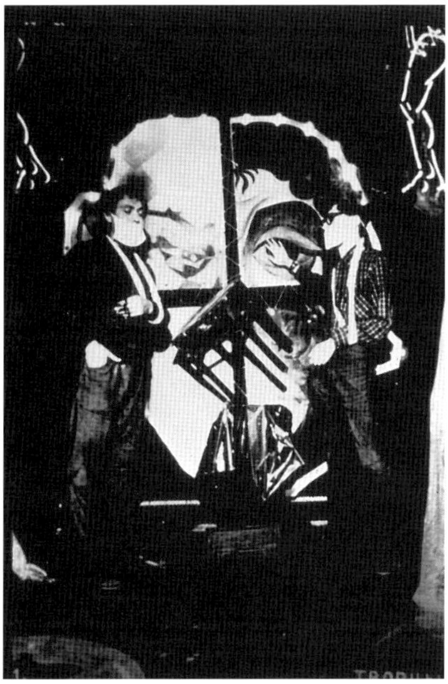

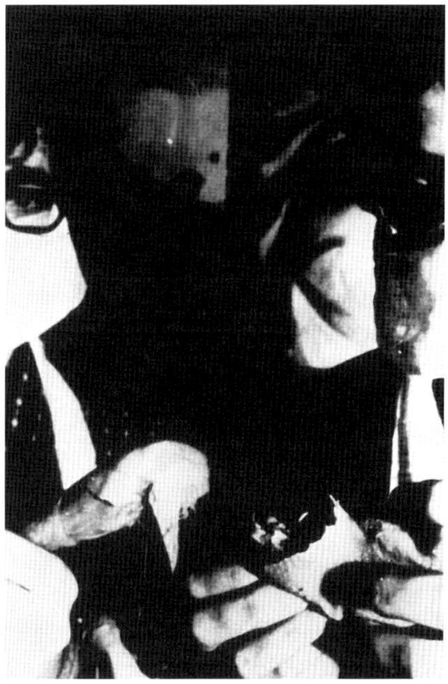

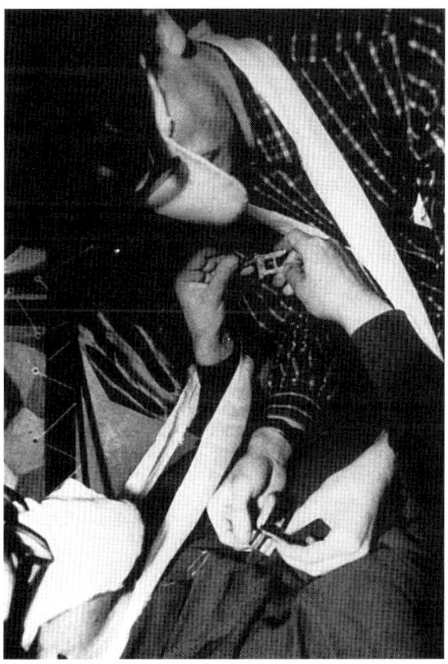

Performance in Paradise was the first unofficial art performance in the Soviet Union. It took place in a Moscow apartment that had been transformed into a closed Soviet "paradise," a parody on the Communist goal of creating a worker's paradise. The room contained a seemingly infinite line of paintings, collages, and slogans. During the performance the audience was locked in a small, windowless room to symbolize the claustrophobic effect of living in Soviet society.

ALEXANDER KOSOLAPOV

Family
1998 (artist's copy of an earlier work dated 1974)
oil on cardboard
50 3/8 x 23 inches
courtesy of the artist

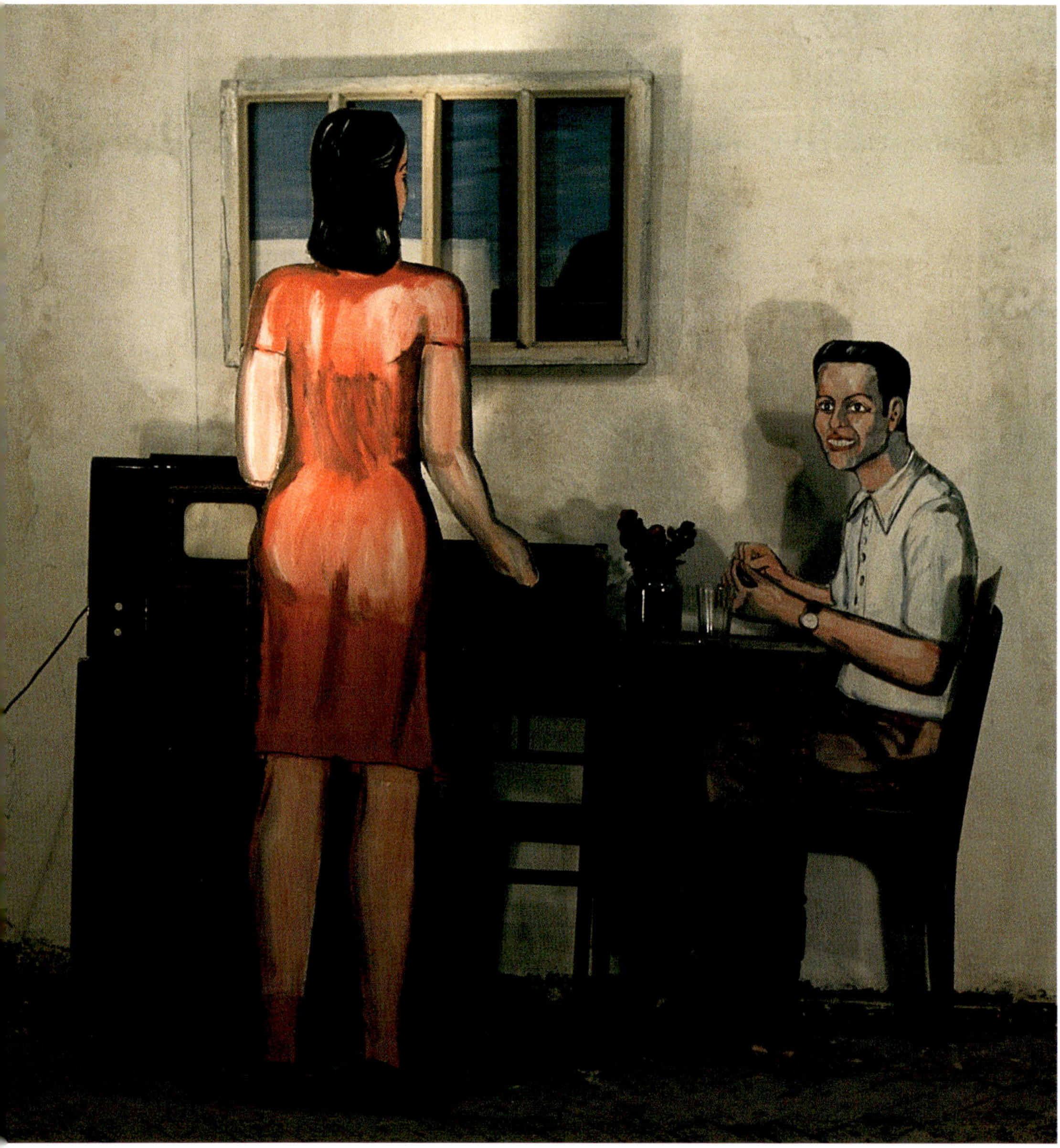

Kosolapov's small, rather crude, cut-out figures seem to exist in a barren world, devoid of anything but superficial emotion.

ALEXANDER KOSOLAPOV

Aurora
1976
oil on board
6 x 7 7/8 inches
courtesy of Alexander Ulikov

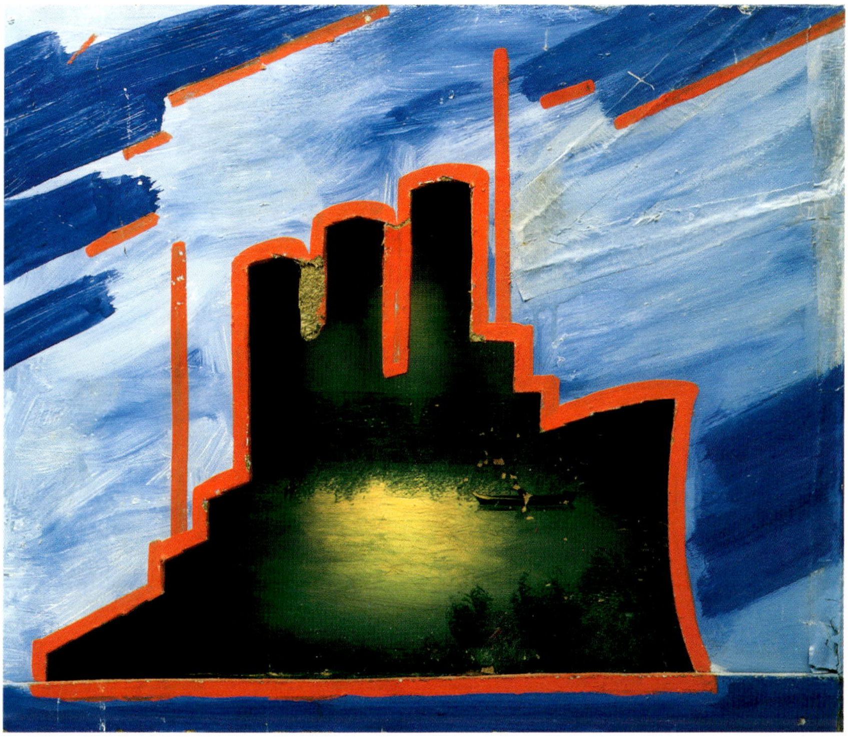

Aurora was intended to be shown in a sots art exhibition organized by Komar and Melamid, but the exhibition never came to pass because of official displeasure. Aurora, a cruiser that played a key role in the October 1917 storming of the winter palace in St. Petersburg by the Bolsheviks, is depicted by Kosolapov as containing a placid, romantic Russian lake. The lake—the romantic dream—seems to be deteriorating, as flakes of paint have fallen off the canvas. The Aurora, a famous symbol of the Russian revolution, is revealed to be at its core only a small and insubstantial canoe that faces a setting sun.

ALEXANDER KOSOLAPOV

Study, Sonny
1975
mixed media
20 1/2 x 18 1/2 x 4 inches
courtesy of Simona and Vyacheslav Sokhransky

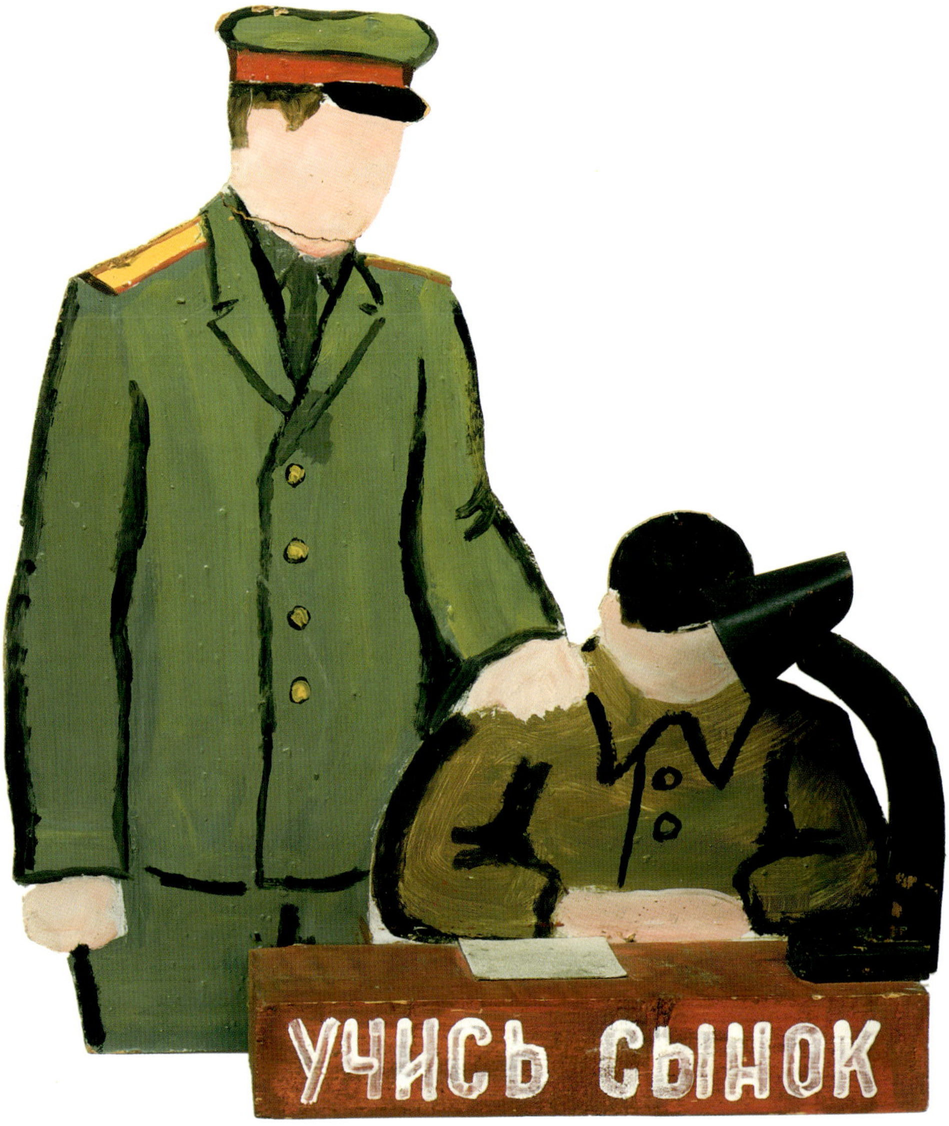

These small cut-out figures were intended to be included in Komar and Melamid's sots art exhibition that was canceled because of government interference. In *Study, Sonny*, Kosolapov represents a faceless young student in a uniform overseen by a faceless adult, also in uniform. The adult's large hand on the shoulder of the student may be a friendly show of support or a reminder of the power of the paternal Soviet system that tried to control all aspects of life.

ALEXANDER KOSOLAPOV

Matches
1974
oil on wood and plaster
20 1/2 x 18 1/2 x 3 15/16 inches
courtesy of the Tsaritsino Museum, Moscow

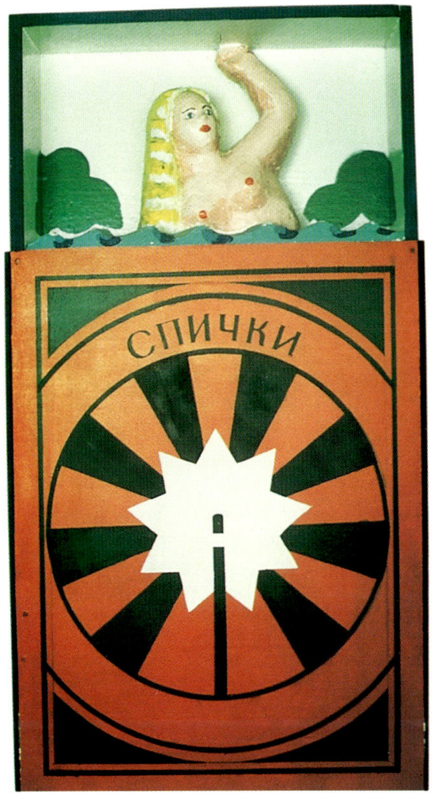

Kosolapov created a fundamental paradox with this very dry matchbox, which contains a painted plaster girl drowning in waves.

ALEXANDER KOSOLAPOV

Swan Lake
1974 and 1998 (from the *Soviet Myth* series)
paint on plaster
32 x 54 inches
courtesy of the artist

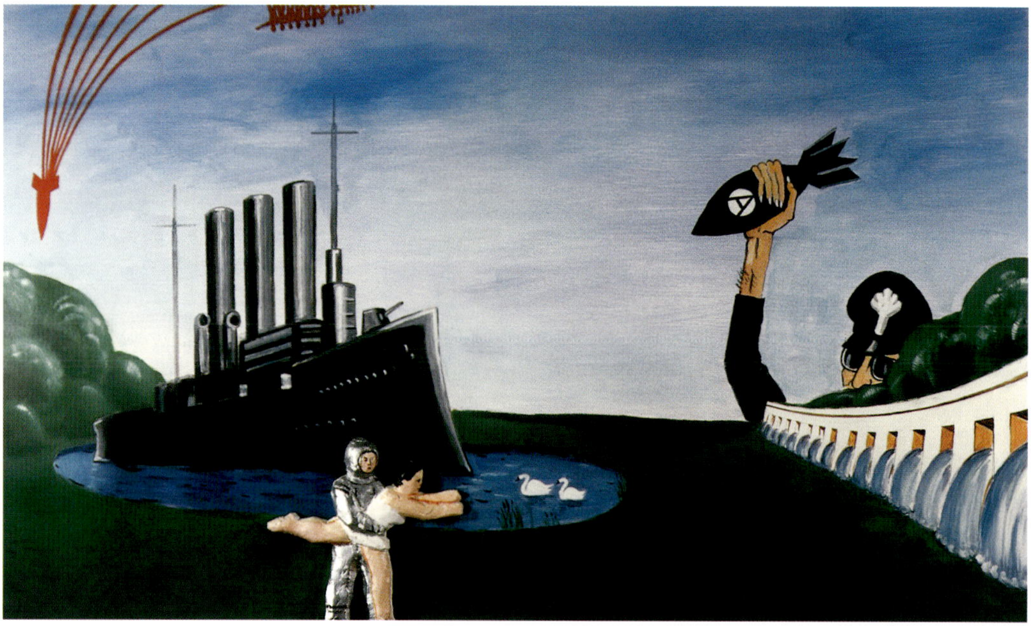

The Soviet Union took as one proof of its political and economic superiority that it produced the world's best dancers, in the tradition of the ballerinas required for classical ballets such as *Swan Lake*, by Russian nineteenth-century composer Peter Tchaikovsky. The other major symbol of Soviet world supremacy was its launch of the first human into space. Kosolapov linked the ballerina and the cosmonaut, both used to create the myth of the superiority of the Soviet system, in an ironic dance.

ALEXANDER KOSOLAPOV

North
1974 (from the *Soviet Myth* series)
mixed media
31 1/2 x 56 inches
courtesy of the artist

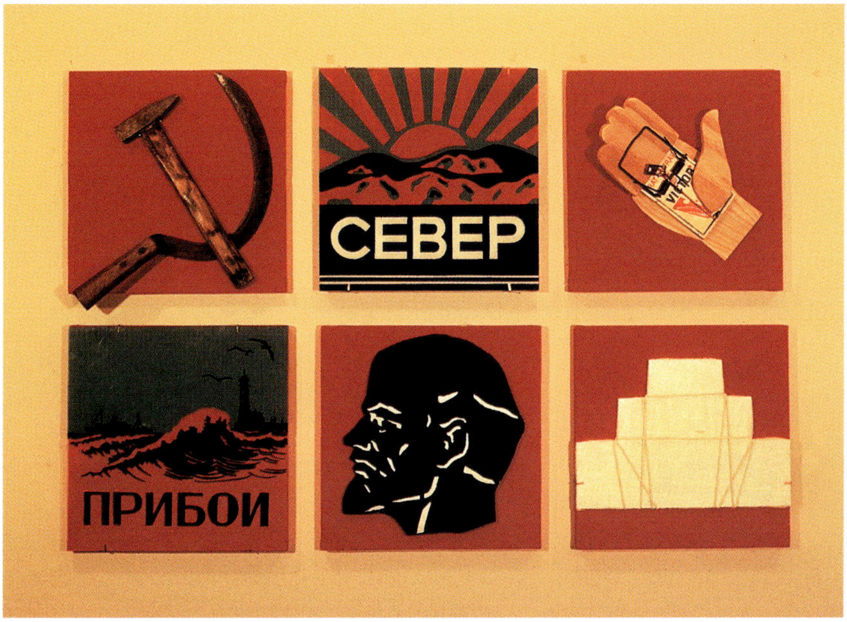

The cigarette trademark North, much like the American brand Lucky Strike, was known to millions of Soviet smokers, but at the same time the term continued to retain its geographic meaning.

LEONID SOKOV

Reconstruction of the 1976 Studio Exhibition in Moscow

which included the following objects:

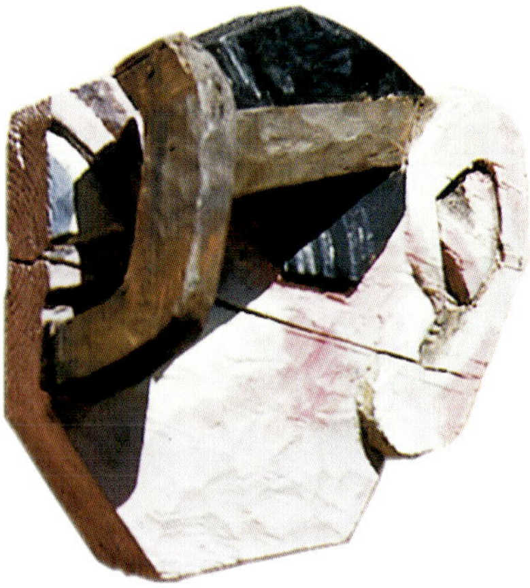

Portrait of Slava Sokhransky
1974
oil paint on wood
13 x 13 1/2 x 5 inches
courtesy of Farideh Cadot, Paris

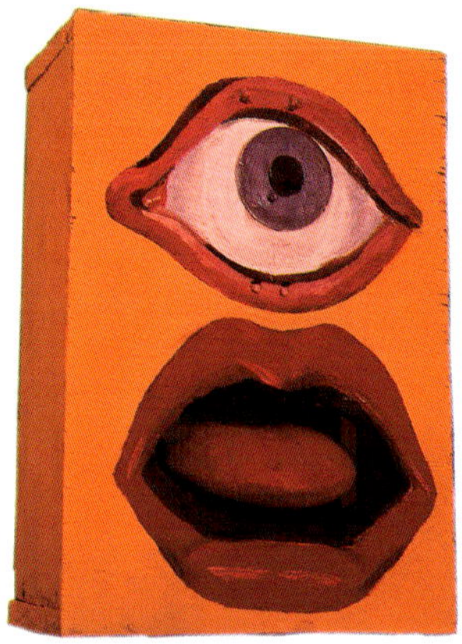

Untitled (Eye and Mouth)
n.d.
painted wood, polystyrene, wind-up mechanism
9 x 6 x 3 inches
courtesy of the Jane Voorhees Zimmerli Art Museum, Rutgers, The State University of New Jersey, The Norton and Nancy Dodge Collection of Nonconformist Art from the Soviet Union

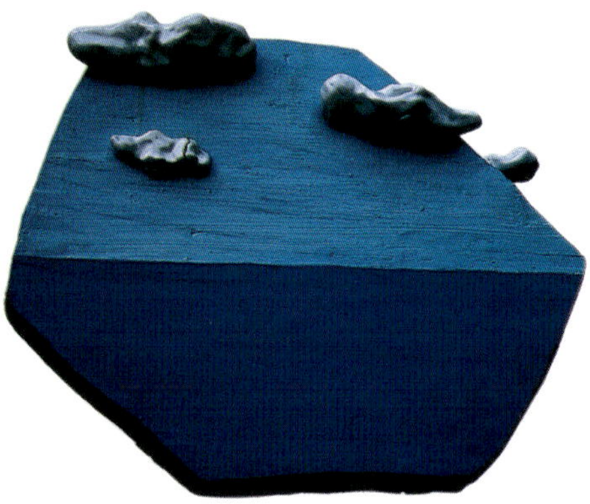

Praila
1973
wood, ceramic, paint
16 x 18 x 5 inches
courtesy of the artist

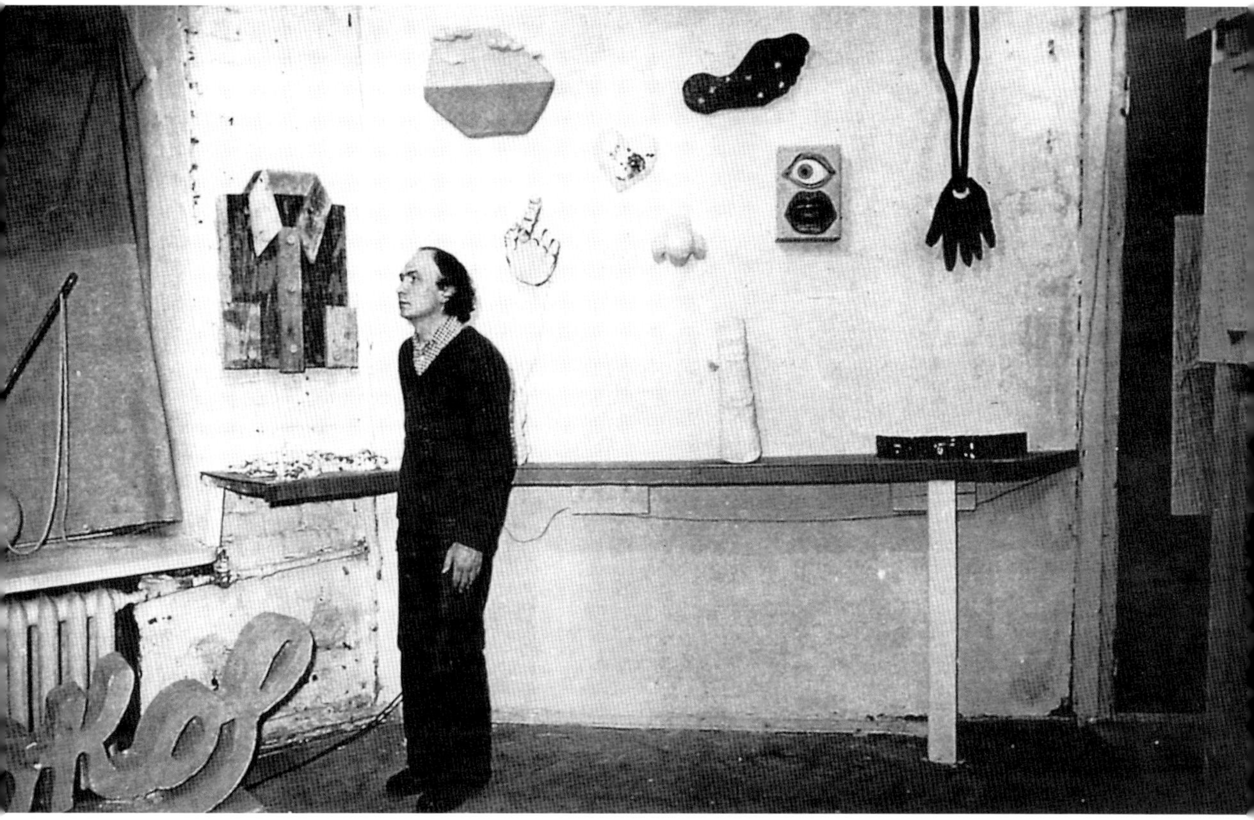

In September 1974, an exhibition of non-official art in a vacant lot in Belyaevo on the outskirts of Moscow was destroyed by government bulldozers. After the international outcry this act created, the government realized it needed to find a compromise in its relationship with nonconformist artists. A city committee (*Gorkom*) was founded to help artists show their work and, at the same time, to control them. Under this committee, a series of studio exhibitions was organized. One of the best of them was Sokov's.

Sokov showed his orientation to pop art, in the tradition of Claes Oldenburg's giant soft sculptures of objects such as electrical plugs, by exhibiting common objects in incompatible materials. His exhibition included, for example, a wooden shirt and a ceramic heart. He also objectified political gestures, such as the threatening finger.

The rough quality of the ceramic or iron objects satirized the poor quality and sloppiness of Soviet industrial production. The primitive mechanical toys allowed him to use folk humor to reveal the flatness of Soviet society.

BORIS ORLOV

Emperor
1975
mixed media, wood, and plaster
34 5/8 x 26 3/4 x 9 7/8 inches
courtesy of the artist

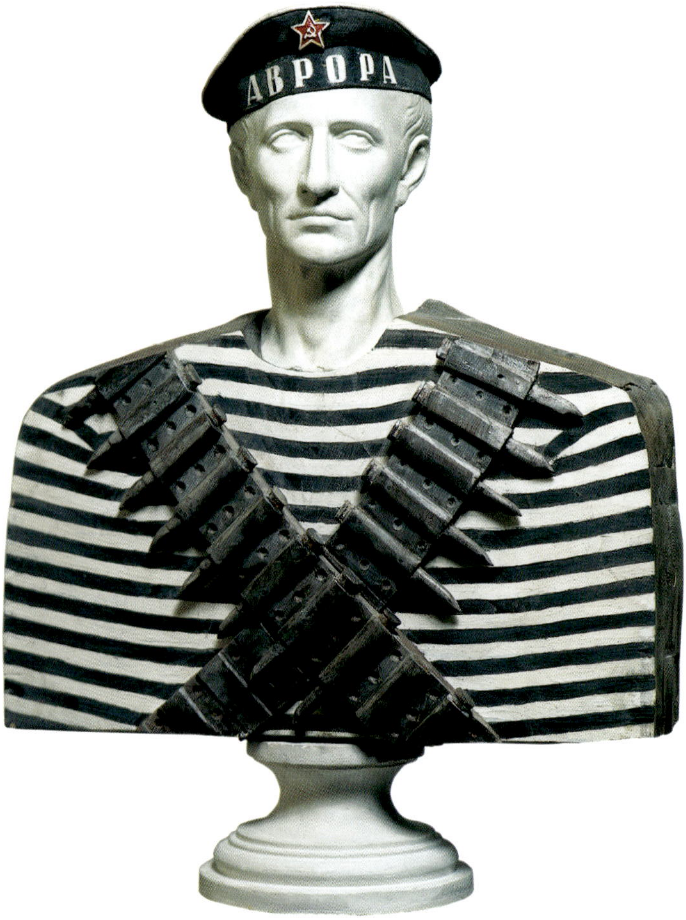

Orlov's favorite hero was a sailor, the most important mythological figure in the Russian Revolution and Soviet history, the very image of its imperial power. Orlov's bust of an emperor is the face from a bust of the ancient Roman emperor and soldier Julius Caesar, represented as a Soviet sailor, his chest crossed by ammunition bandoleers. He is wearing a beret emblazoned with the hammer and sickle of the Soviet Union and the word "Aurora," designating the famous battleship that gave the signal for the storming of the winter palace by the Bolsheviks in October of 1917.

The bust of the sailor sits on a marble pedestal, as did the portrait busts of Roman emperors. Moscow had long thought of itself as "the third Rome," the rightful heir to the great Christian-Roman empire of the ancient world. The sailor, the hero of the Russian revolution, is transformed by the artist into a Roman emperor, the ruler of the third Rome.

BORIS ORLOV

Avenue of Heroes
1975
mixed media
31 1/8 x 66 15/16 inches each panel
courtesy of the artist

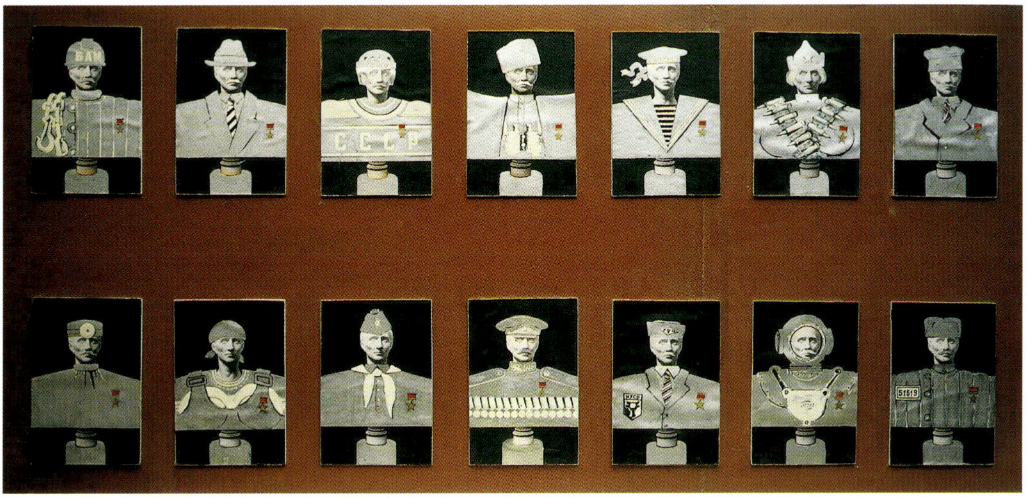

Orlov reduces the portraits of official heroes, mounted on the marble bases associated with ancient Roman marble portrait busts, to bemedaled, beribboned chests groaning under the weight of officialdom. But the honors are hollow ones—the heroes play at awarding each other with meaningless medals.

BORIS ORLOV

The Generals of Russian Science and Culture
1990 (artist's copy of an earlier work dated 1982)
mixed media
6 panels, 23 5/8 x 17 5/16 inches each
courtesy of the artist

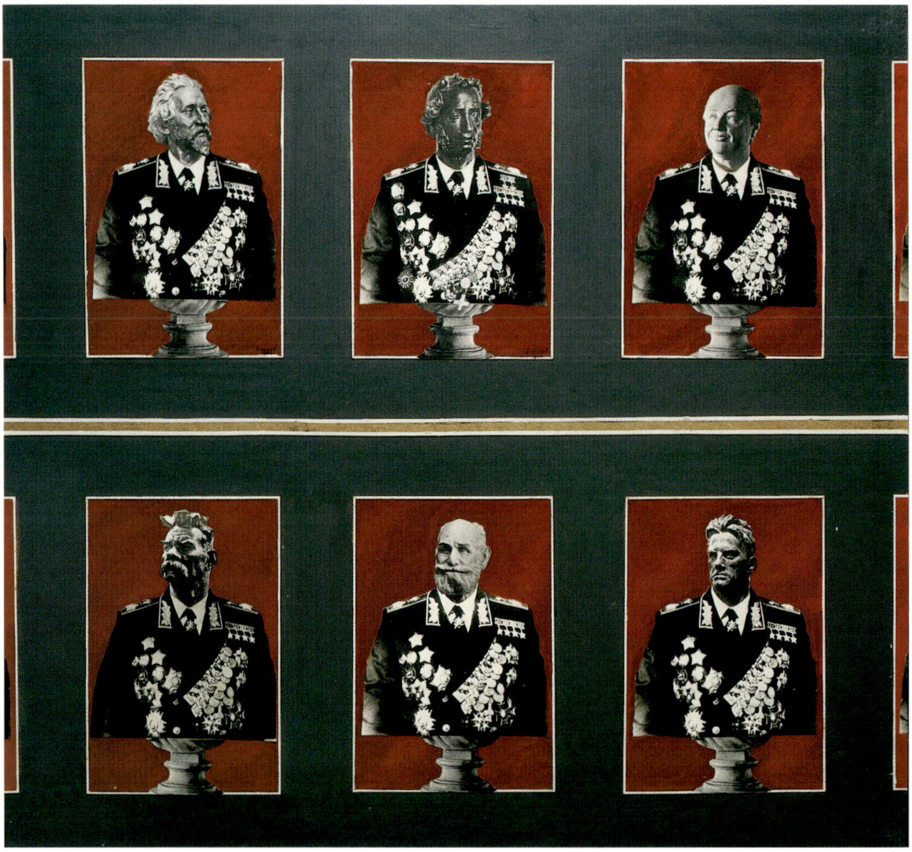

Orlov's 1980s works parodied the military paranoia of the later part of the regime of Leonid Brezhnev. Here, the leaders of culture and science are made into generals, with uniforms and medals.

ERIC BULATOV

Red Horizons
1971–72
oil on canvas
55 1/8 x 70 7/8 inches
courtesy of Galerie Clara Maria Sels, Düsseldorf, Germany

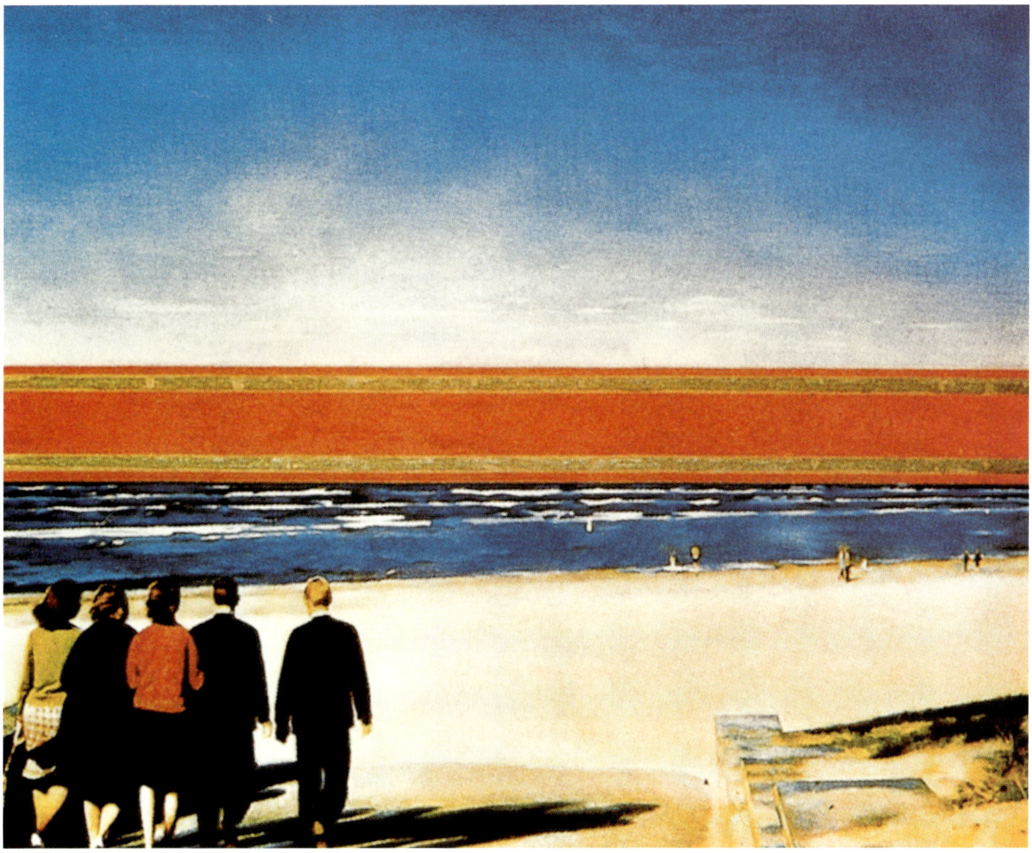

Bulatov's many layers of space represent a structure of the world that includes various levels of external and inner life. His paintings do not intend to satirize Soviet reality, but show, instead, the limitation of political power to affect the human soul. Soviet symbols associated with the corridors of power, such as an official red carpet shown here on the horizon, are depicted with realistic exactitude but are only a superficial level of reality.

ERIC BULATOV

Exit-No Exit
1973
gouache on paper
10 x 10 inches
courtesy of Anatoly Bekkerman, ABA Gallery, New York

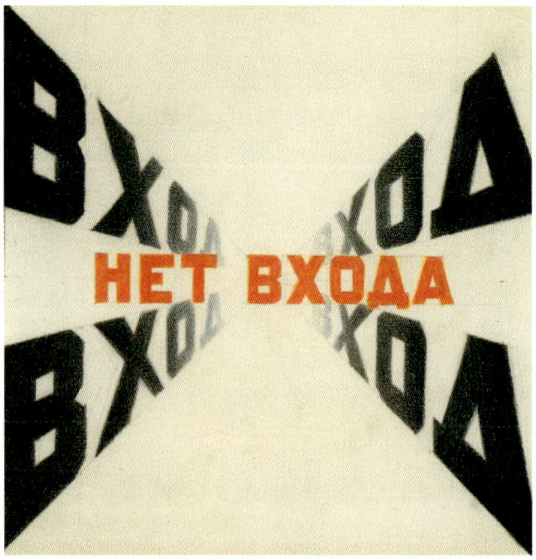

Using a type face and the colors favored by the abstract geometric art movements of suprematism and constructivism, which flourished in Russia in the early decades of the twentieth century, Bulatov expresses the contradictions inherent in daily life in the Soviet Union. He places "exits" in seemingly infinite space, but at the potential vanishing point, the red "no exit" flashes.

opposite page
Roshal-Fedorov inserted his portrait as the face of a saint in this painting done on panel in the Byzantine style of Russian Orthodox icons. On the cover of the red gospel the saint holds in one hand, the artist replaced the religious message that would traditionally be found there with the emphatic Communist slogan, "Will Give the Coal Above Plan!"

Under the Soviet economic system, factories were assigned inflexible production goals based on a "five year plan" rather than on market demand. The message of this painting is that Communist ideology, which criticized religion as "the opiate of the people," had replaced Christianity's aphorisms with its own vacuous slogans.

MIKHAIL ROSHAL-FEDOROV

Will Give the Coal Above Plan!
1974
oil on wood
31 1/2 x 23 5/8 inches
courtesy of the artist

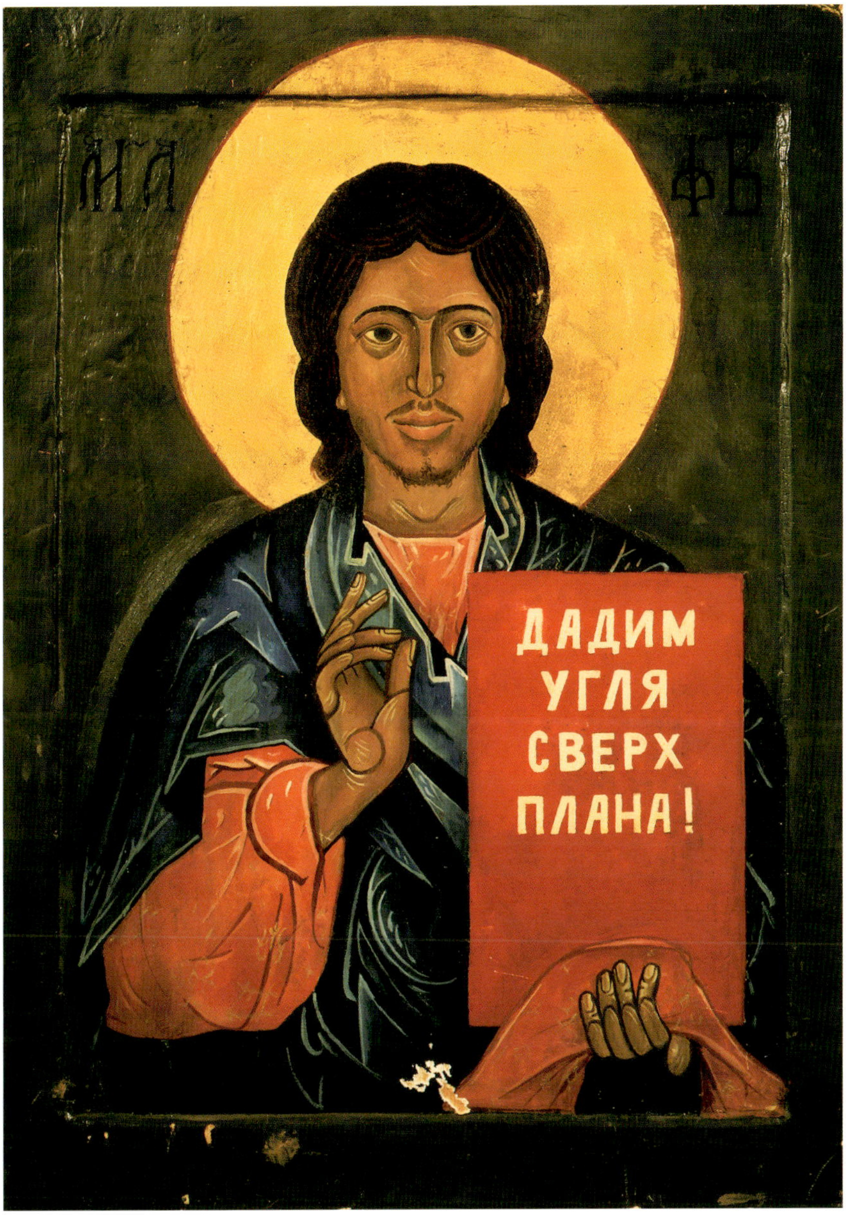

THE NEST

(GENADY DONSKOY, MIKHAIL ROSHAL-FEDOROV, VICTOR SKERSIS)

Pump the Red Pump!
1975
mixed media
47 1/4 x 31 1/2 inches
courtesy of Mikhail Roshal-Fedorov

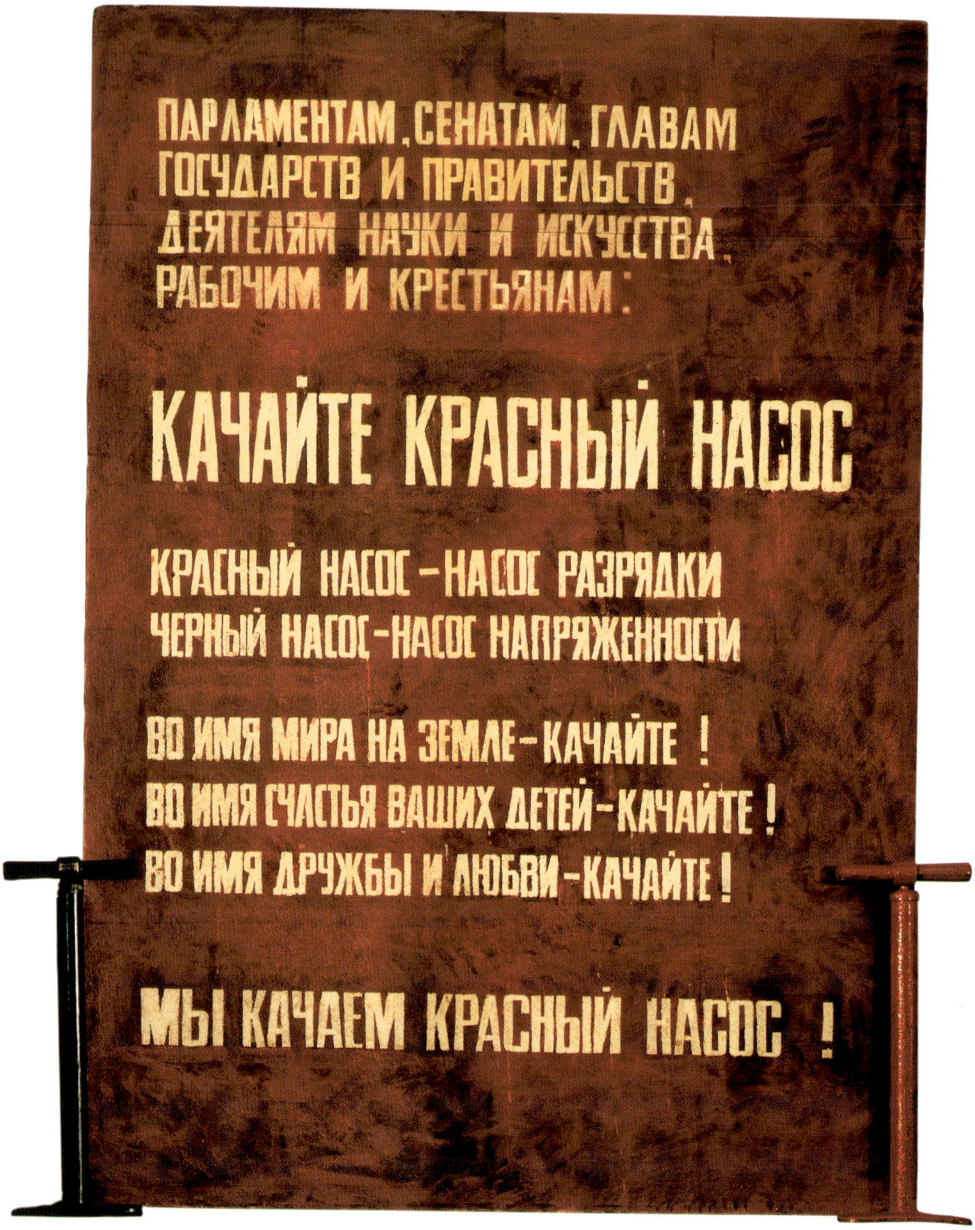

The group called The Nest, formed by some of Komar and Melamid's students, took a nihilistic attitude to all social, religious, and artistic values. *Pump the Red Pump!* comments on the absurdity of the Soviet style of work and of Communist ideological demands.

The text is an inane appeal to world parliaments, governments, scientists, artists, workers, and "peasants" to pump the red pump, not the black pump, which is the pump of tensions. It ends with a ritual-like chant that mimics a Christian prayer: "In the name of peace on earth, pump! In the name of the happiness of our children, pump! In the name of friendship and love, pump! We are pumping the red pump!"

★SOTS ART AT HOME

BY THE MID-1970S, SEVERAL IMPORTANT SOTS ARTISTS HAD EMIGRATED TO NEW YORK, FORCED OUT BY INCREASINGLY REPRESSIVE GOVERNMENT POLICIES TOWARD UNDERGROUND ART. **ALEXANDER KOSOLAPOV**, **VITALY KOMAR**, **ALEXANDER MELAMID**, **LEONID SOKOV**, AND **VAGRICH BAKHCHANYAN** GATHERED IN NEW YORK AND THERE, ON POP ART'S HOME GROUND, SOTS ART ENTERED A NEW PHASE. AS IS COMMON FOR ÉMIGRÉS, THE FIRST ENCOUNTER OF THESE ARTISTS WITH THE REALITY OF AMERICA WAS DISAPPOINTING AND PROVOKED A KIND OF NOSTALGIA, EVEN IN ARTISTS INTENSELY CRITICAL OF THE SOVIET SYSTEM. THESE ARTISTS WERE ABLE TO INTERPRET THEIR COMPLICATED FEELINGS OF NOSTALGIA FOR CHILDHOOD MEMORIES AND NAIVE EXPECTATIONS ABOUT THE WEST THROUGH THE IRONY OF SOTS ART.

& IN EXILE

Komar and Melamid's 1981–82 *Nostalgic Socialist Realism* series, which includes *The Origin of Socialist Realism*, was vital in defining this new phase of sots art. At a distance from the Soviet Union, they were able to embrace its life and art as a historical phase that would never occur again. Anticipating the collapse of the Soviet Union, they created this series of paintings penetrated by the spirit of death. At once subversive and nostalgic, they used the painting techniques that characterized the "high academicism" of nineteenth-century European art to satirize the representational styles favored by totalitarian art.

Another characteristic of these sots artists in exile was their combination of the sign systems of American society and the world they had left behind, to satirize both. Alexander Kosolapov's ability to combine the icons of American consumerism and of Soviet ideology gave rise to such emblematic works as *Coca-Cola*. In this work, he combined the slogan and trademark of Coca-Cola, the symbol of the American consumerist, economic empire, and the profile of Lenin, the most famous figure of the Russian revolution and the founder of the Soviet political empire. Leonid Sokov's personages, which have the crude forms of folk toys, also combine the two cultures. *Lips and Mustaches* equates Marilyn Monroe's voluptuous lips and Joseph Stalin's bushy mustache as symbols of American and Soviet cultures.

Those artists who remained in Moscow, such as **Boris Orlov**, **Rostislav Lebedev**, and **Grisha Bruskin**, developed complex systems of representation that embodied social, moral, and mythological codes of meaning. Lebedev's cards, for example, represented various nations and the symbols of their political power as part of a card game. Grisha Bruskin, always mindful of his Jewish heritage, included religious symbols and metaphysical ideas in his systems for classifying Soviet officialdom.

VITALY KOMAR AND ALEXANDER MELAMID

The Origin of Socialist Realism
1982 (from the series *Nostalgic Socialist Realism*)
mixed media on cardboard
39 7/8 x 32 inches
courtesy of Neil K. Rector

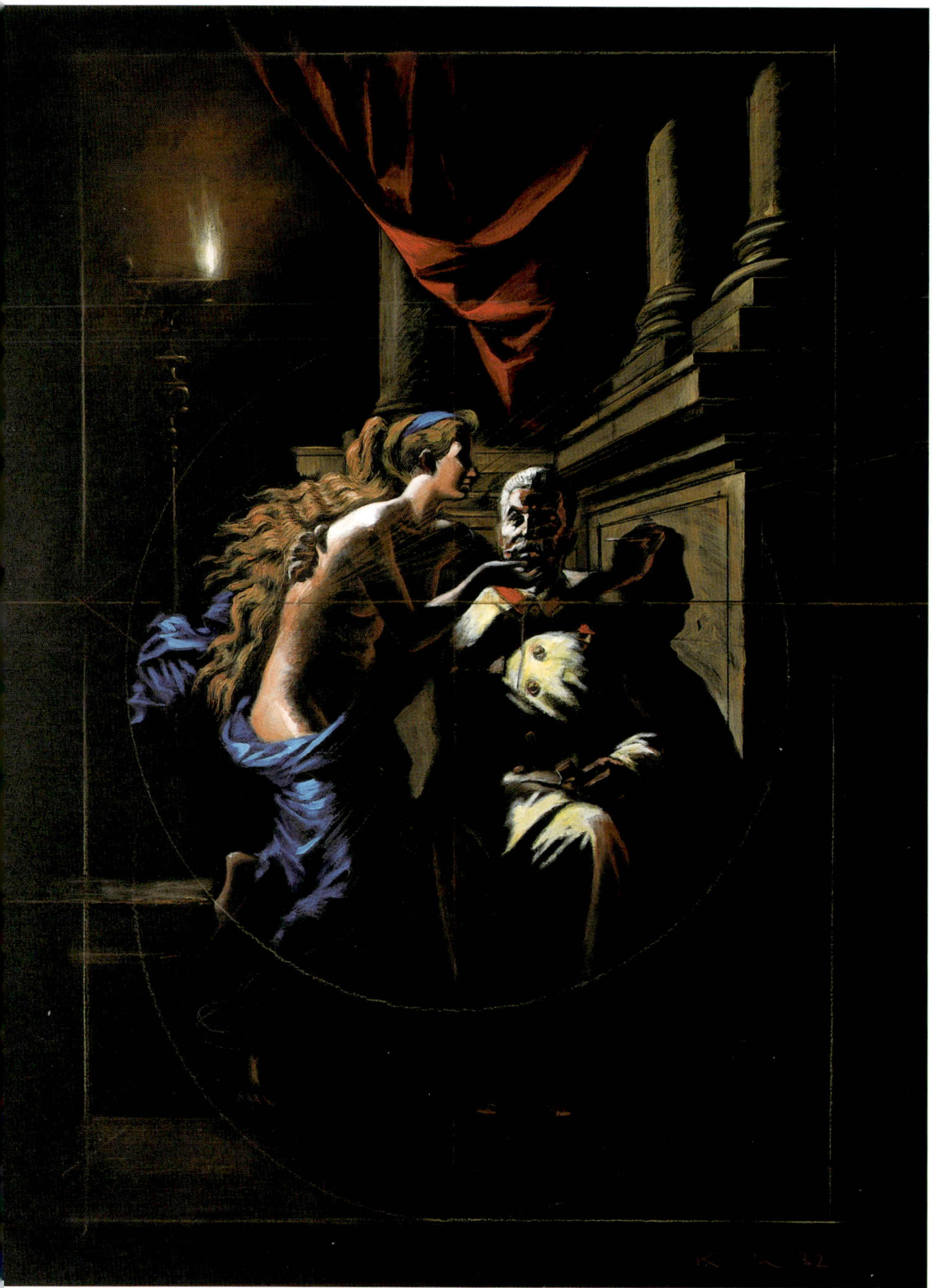

Komar and Melamid's 1981–82 *Nostalgic Socialist Realism* series, of which this painting is a part, was vital in defining the New York phase of sots art. Komar and Melamid used the techniques of high academicism—enormous scale, realistic figures, grandiose subjects, and a highly finished surface—to satirize the overblown representational style of official Soviet art.

Soviet socialist realism presented official ideology and inspirational messages in a realistic style. *The Origin of Socialist Realism* presents Soviet dictator Joseph Stalin, who ruled the Soviet Union from the death of its founder, Vladimir Ilyich Lenin, in 1924 until his own in 1953. Stalin is seen with a muse—his inspiration—in a pose used by nineteenth-century academic painters to present great philosophers of the ancient and modern world. The muse traces the shadow of Stalin's profile—the origin of Soviet realism, the only sanctioned art of the Soviet Union.

During his life, Stalin was hailed as a "universal genius," as a "shining sun," or "the staff of life." He arranged to be the hero of cult propaganda in the form of busts, paintings, statues, and icons that enhanced his status and absolute power. This painting verges on the surrealistic with its gigantic architectural background swathed in symbolic red drapery, evocative of the power of the unconscious and the erotic.

Presenting the muse, or pure inspiration, as the source of official painting—and perhaps of Stalin's cruel repression of the Russian people through political assassinations and internment in Siberian forced labor camps—was an ironic statement about an art—and a political system—that was prescribed and didactic. At the same time, the idea of Stalin in the presence of this muse-goddess captured the repressed but lingering love of many Soviet citizens for Stalin as a potent leader at the height of his powers of erotic seduction. Themes of death and eroticism symbolized the mystic power of Stalin as cruel patriarch and permeated his dark and bloody deeds.

VITALY KOMAR AND ALEXANDER MELAMID

Revolution in Boston
1979
banner and model of the installation in the Boston School of Visual Arts
linen, paint, cloth, and wood
24 x 36 x 36 inches
courtesy of the artists

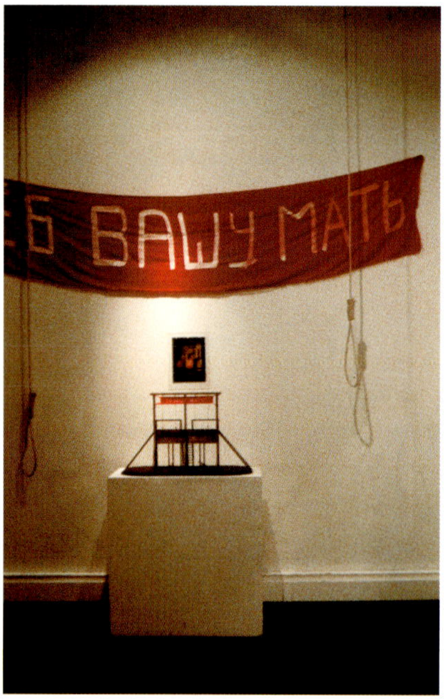

Revolution in Boston was created by the artists and their students at the Boston School of Visual Arts. Komar and Melamid were always trying to find the common points in Soviet, European, and American history. For this installation and performance, the artists started with the Boston Tea Party incident from early American history, when American patriots dumped tea from a ship into Boston Harbor in 1773 to protest repressive English taxes on tea. Komar and Melamid inserted, into this scene of the American Revolution, a twentieth-century Soviet slogan and traditional Russian insult (*blat*), and a guillotine from the period of the French Revolution against the monarchy in 1789.

opposite page
This image of the famous ancient statue, the Venus de Milo, has been altered by Komar and Melamid to include her missing arms, one holding the hammer, the other the sickle which, with the red star, were the most common symbols of the Soviet Union.

Venus de Milo
1983
oil on canvas
72 x 48 inches
courtesy of Neil K. Rector

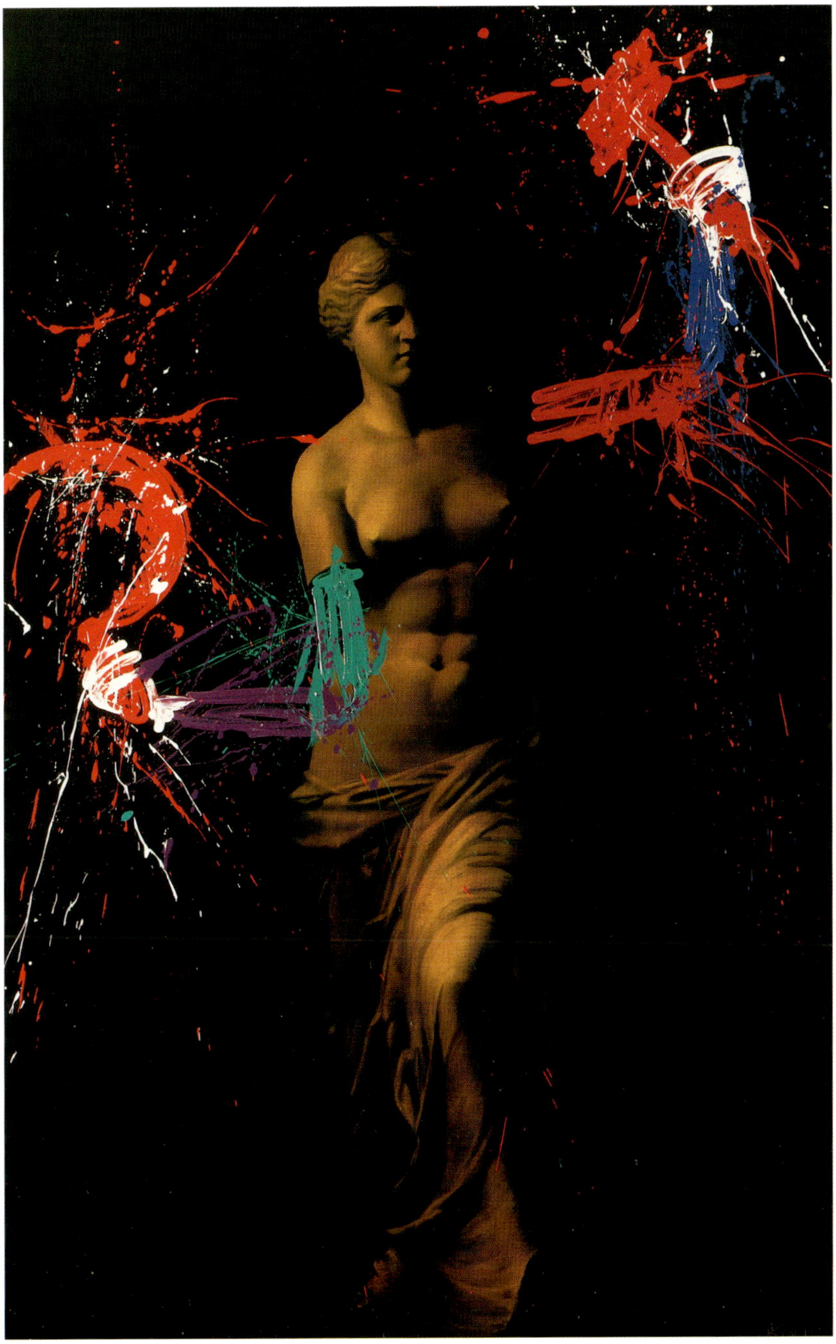

Komar and Melamid's painting of the end of the *third* world war shows a nineteenth-century romantic depiction of a Soviet soldier holding a giant sword in one hand and wearing a swirling, sensuous red cape.

The figure is well known to Russians from a monument placed in Treptov Park in Berlin, Germany shortly after the end of World War II to commemorate the Soviet Union's role in the defeat of Hitler. On the arm of this larger-than-life figure of the Soviet soldier—liberator of Germany—the artists substituted a black child swathed in stars and stripes for the German girl who appeared in the original sculpture, to parody the idea that a Soviet soldier would be the conqueror-liberator of America, too.

When this painting was originally exhibited, it was accompanied by a real cradle broken by a steel beam, to emphasize the double meaning of the Soviet "liberator's" role.

VITALY KOMAR AND ALEXANDER MELAMID

The Third World War Ends
1982–83
oil on canvas
48 x 40 inches
courtesy of the Sloane Gallery of Art, Denver

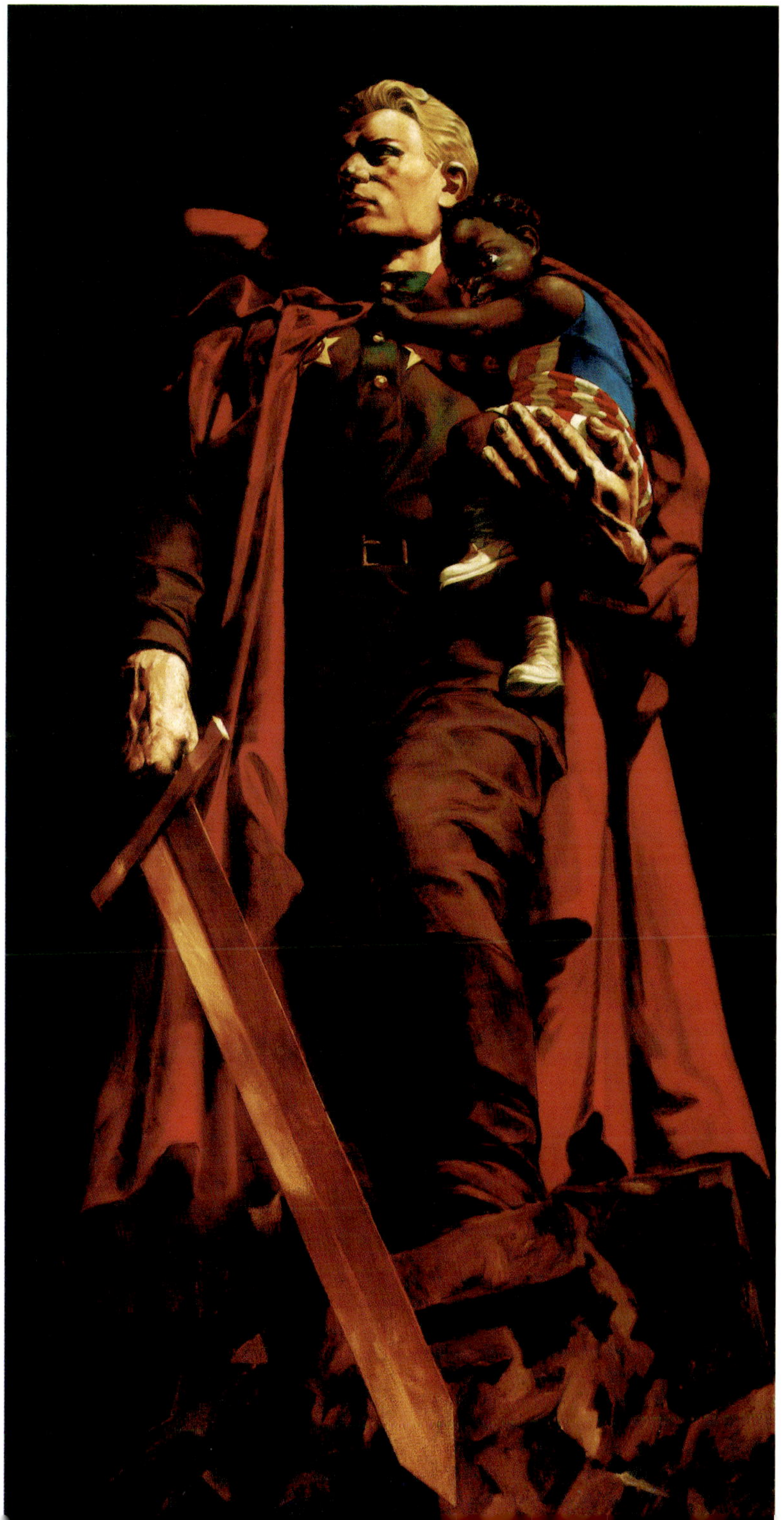

VITALY KOMAR AND ALEXANDER MELAMID

Double Self Portrait
1985–86
mixed media
2 panels, each 60 x 72 inches
courtesy of the Sloane Gallery of Art, Denver

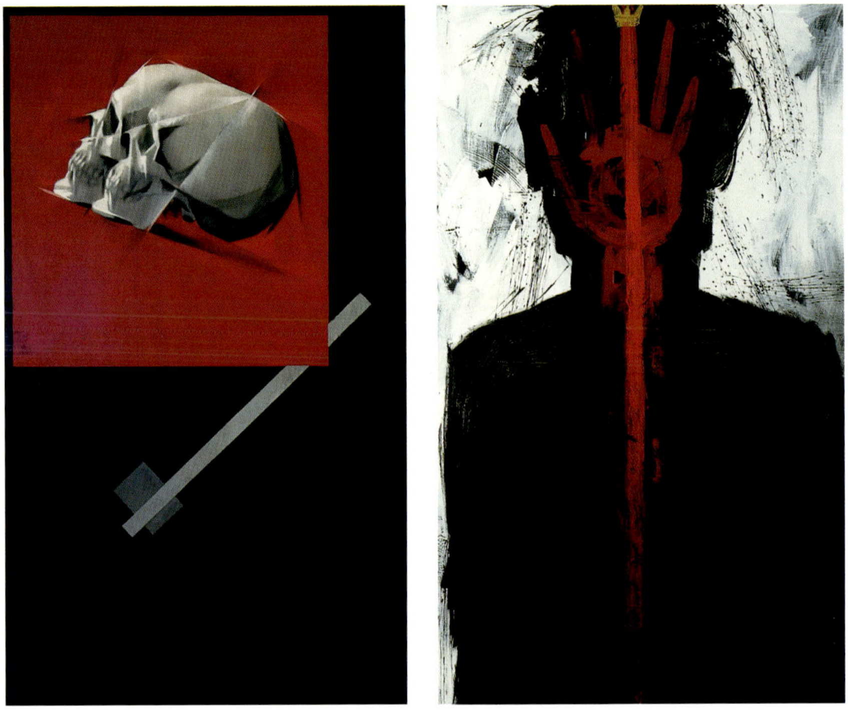

The dark, symbolic set of self-portraits seems to imply the negation of individualism, while at the same time its forms harken back to the geometric abstraction of the suprematist and constructivist artistic styles that predominated during the early days of the Russian Revolution, in the first decade of this century.

ALEXANDER KOSOLAPOV

Coca-Cola
1980
acrylic on canvas
78 3/4 x 118 1/8 inches
courtesy of Drs. Irene and Alex Valger

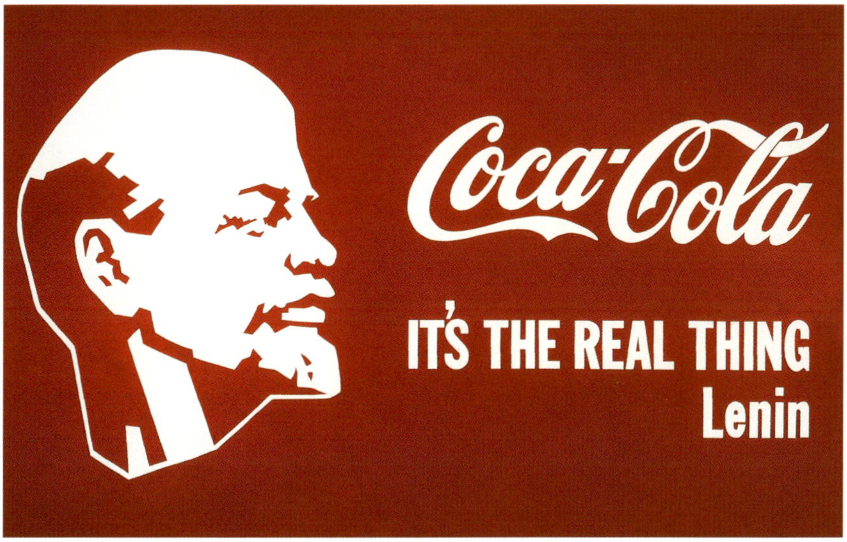

Kosolapov juxtaposed a profile of Vladimir Ilyich Lenin, the founder of the Communist state in Russia, and the Coca-Cola trademark and slogan. In addition to being an ironic comparison of the Soviet Union, for which ideology was the "real thing," and America, where a soft drink reigned, perhaps Kosolapov intended to remind us that Lenin's vision was the "real thing" because it truly changed the world.

ALEXANDER KOSOLAPOV

Thwip
1985
acrylic on canvas
72 x 60 inches
courtesy of a private collection

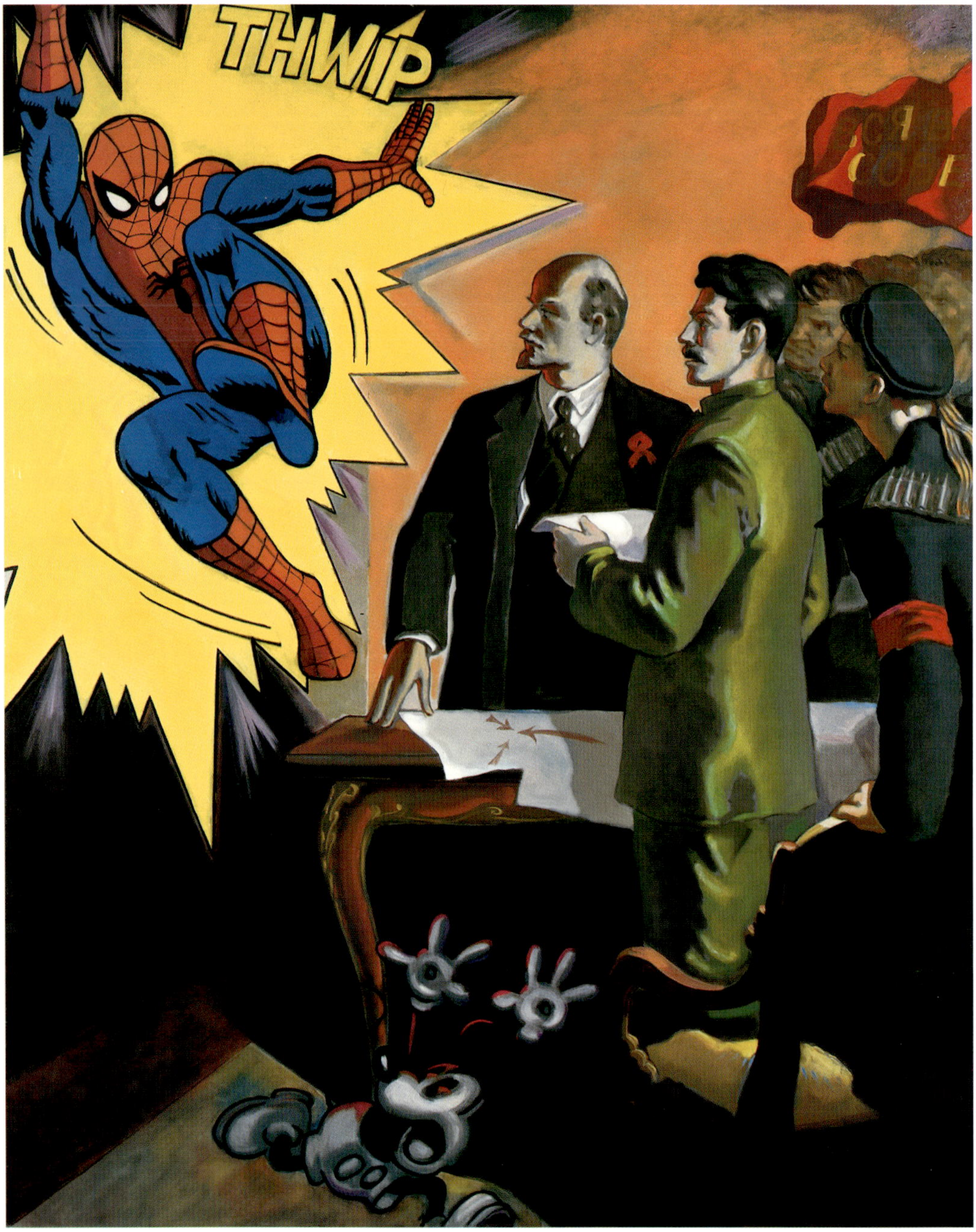

Using the cartoon style favored by some American pop artists, particularly Roy Lichtenstein, Kosolapov depicts Vladimir Ilyich Lenin's strategic planning meeting for the Russian revolution, interrupted by a super hero—Spiderman—who arrives in a lightening bolt with the onomatopoetic word "Thwip," signifying the sound his arrival makes. Mickey Mouse below the table flees in terror.

The man in the green suit is the young Joseph Stalin, who took control of the Soviet Union after Lenin's death in 1924. Even though Stalin was not present at these kinds of revolutionary strategy meetings, he made sure he was inserted into later paintings to give the impression that he had been central to the Communist victory over forces loyal to the monarchy.

Lenin and his advisors are depicted in a typical Soviet realist style, surrounded by brave sailors wearing red armbands and ammunition bandoleers over their shoulders, and with a noble red banner bearing a revolutionary slogan unfurling in the background. There is an absurdity to the confrontation between Lenin, the superhero of the Russian revolution depicted in a scene familiar from many Russian propaganda paintings, and Spiderman, depicted as an exaggerated fictional character from American popular culture.

ALEXANDER KOSOLAPOV

Malevich Sold Here
1989
acrylic on canvas
52 x 80 inches
courtesy of the artist

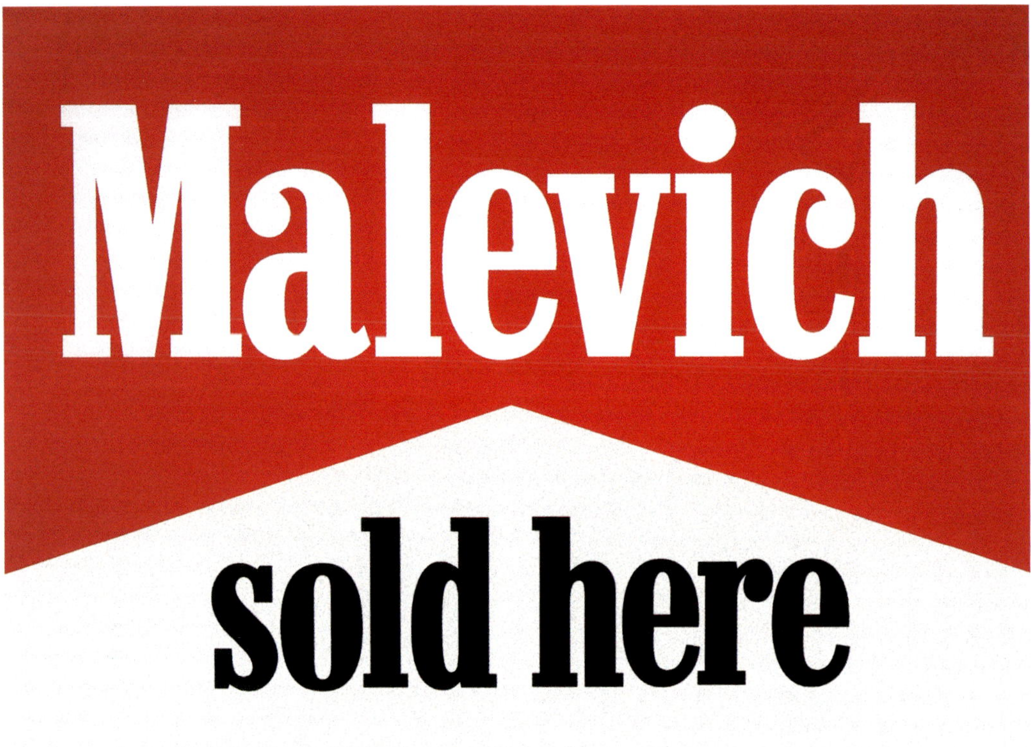

In 1915 Kazimir Malevich founded a movement of Russian abstract geometrical painting he called suprematism. Suprematism and constructivism, another geometric abstract movement in art and architecture founded at about the same time in Russia, were in favor at the time of the Russian Revolution. These avant-garde art forms were deemed appropriate for a revolution that intended to change the world's ideas about the organization of all aspects of society. When Soviet politicians decided against modern art, Malevich and his art were doomed. He died in poverty and oblivion.

Kosolapov used the strongly colored, abstract geometric forms of the Marlboro cigarette package to make a visual pun about Malevich's art, which used similar forms and colors. The word "sold" in the title of the work may have a double meaning, typical for Kosolapov's art. Malevich's work has been sold for the high prices in America that he never achieved in Russia during his life. At the same time, the title may refer to the idea that Malevich's artistic ideals have been "sold out" to or defeated by the American consumerism represented by cigarette advertising.

LEONID SOKOV

Meeting of Two Sculptures [Lenin and Giacometti]
1990
bronze
18 1/8 x 15 3/8 x 5 1/2 inches
courtesy of Drs. Irene and Alex Valger

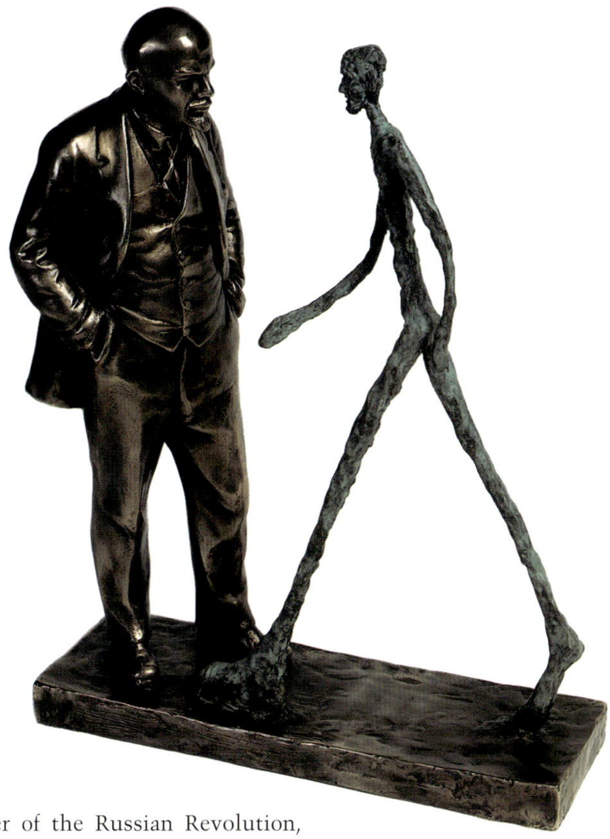

The leader of the Russian Revolution, Vladimir Ilyich Lenin, meets a stylized man in the style of twentieth-century Swiss sculptor Alberto Giacometti. There is a visual pun in the contrast between the stocky Lenin and the attenuated figure typical of Giacometti's style. The Giacometti-like figure strides firmly towards a frowning Lenin, perhaps to indicate the clash between modern art and Soviet ideology that would have repressed artists like Giacometti—and Sokov himself.

LEONID SOKOV

Lips and Moustaches Icon
1990
oil on canvas
80 x 80 inches
collection of Wayne F. Yakes, M.D.
courtesy of the Sloane Gallery of Art, Denver

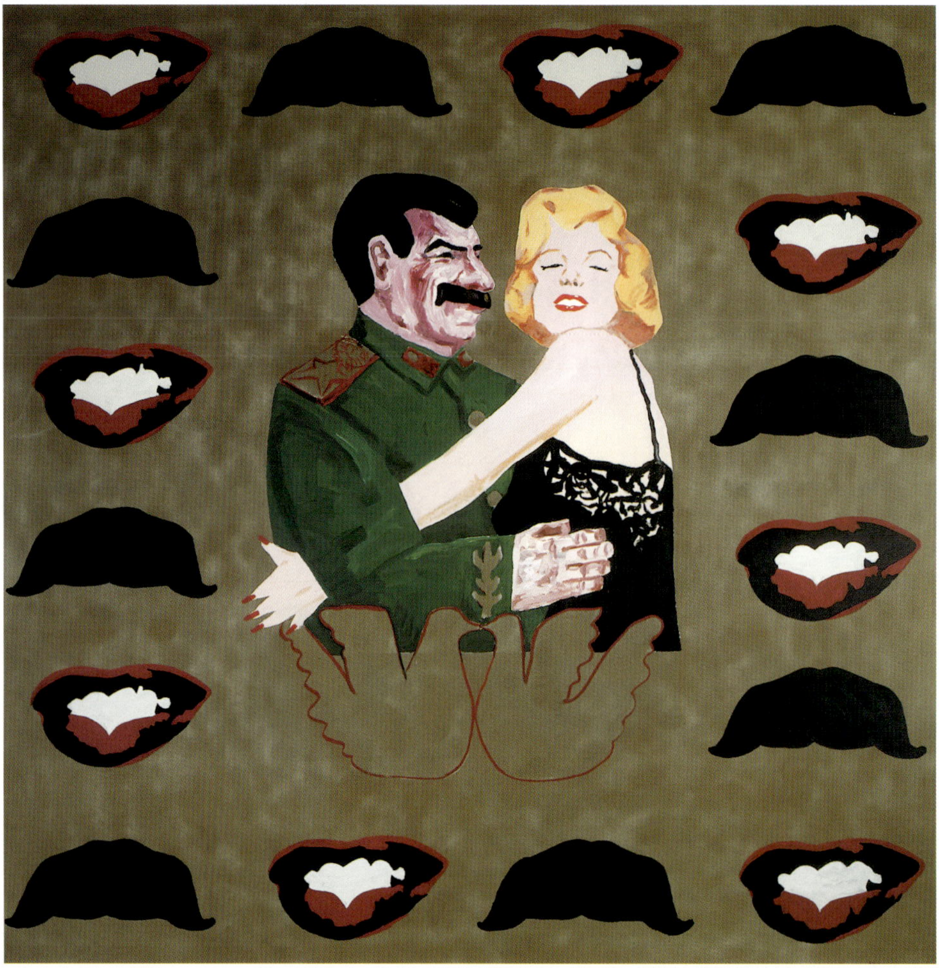

Sokov's forms are based on folk toys (*lubok*). *Lips and Moustaches* shows Soviet dictator Joseph Stalin and American film star Marilyn Monroe as if they were crude wooden toys, locked in an embrace, framed by multiple images of her famous toothy smile and his equally well-known bushy black moustache. *Lips and Moustaches* equates Monroe's voluptuous lips and Stalin's bushy moustache as symbols of American and Soviet cultures.

By combining Stalin with an American popular culture icon, Sokov moved a Soviet ideological figure into the realm of popular entertainment, America's most pervasive export to the world.

LEONID SOKOV

Stalin and Hitler
1983
painted wood, motors
44 x 35 x 10 inches
courtesy of David Thickman

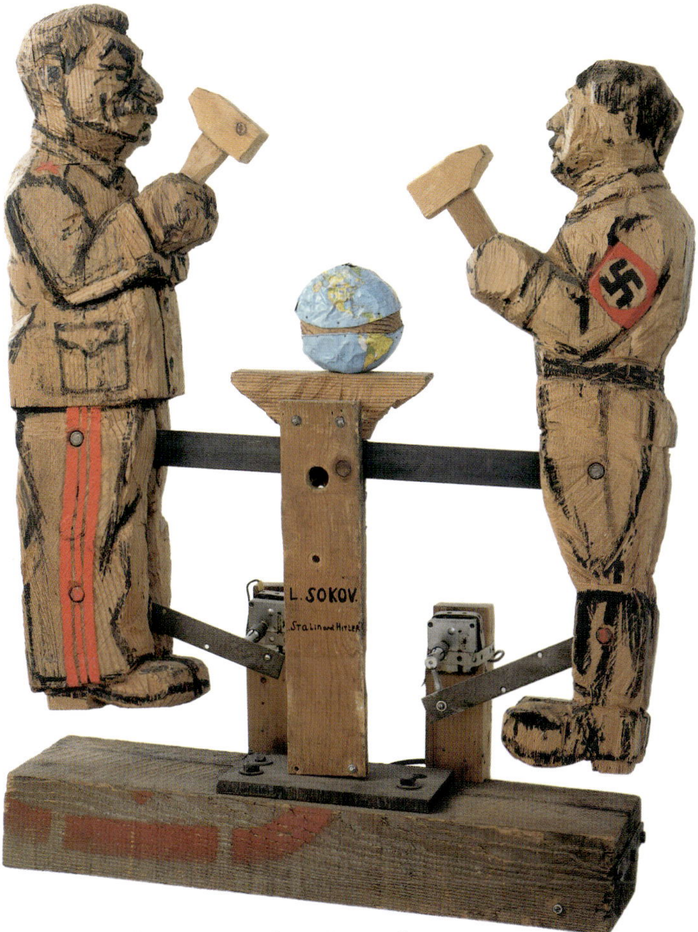

The Soviet dictator, Joseph Stalin, and the German Nazi dictator, Adolph Hitler, are depicted as opposing figures who alternately batter the world with hammers in this kinetic wooden folk toy.

GRISHA BRUSHIN

The Birth of the Hero
1988
photographs from a performance in Moscow at the Kashirka Exhibition Hall
courtesy of the artist

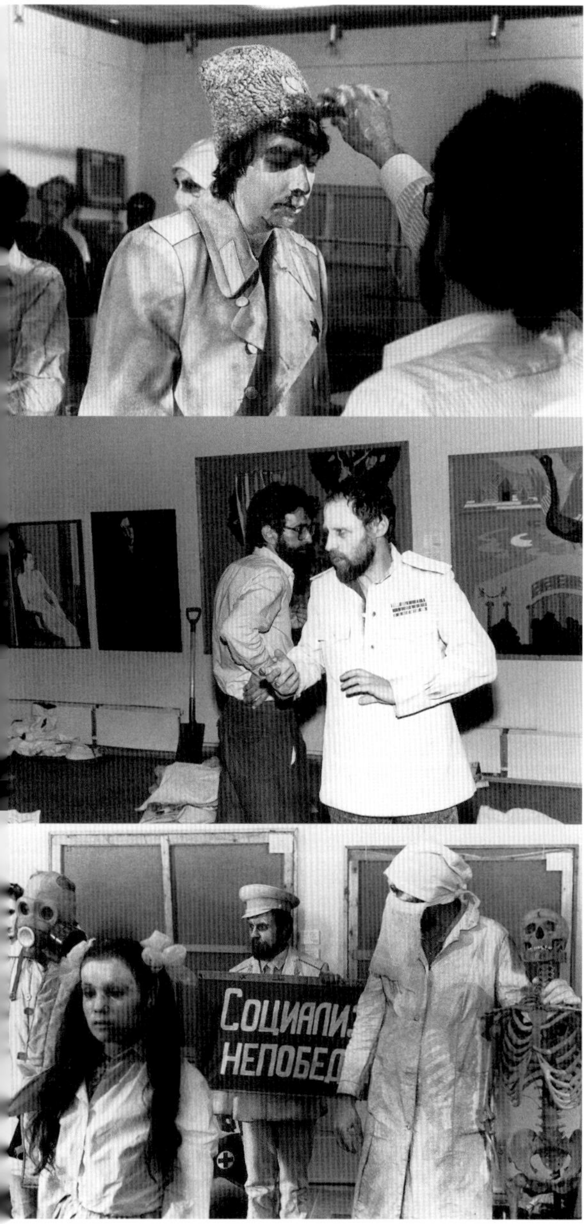

Artists Boris Orlov, Evgeni Vakhtangov, Vadim Zakharov, Yuri Albert, Joseph Bakshtein, artist and poet Dmitri Prigov, poet Lev Rubenstein, and musicians Mark Pekarsky and Vladimir Tarasov participated in this performance in Moscow. Costumes, white cloth wrappings, and makeup transformed the participants into the white plaster figures in Bruskin's paintings.

Bruskin, armed with a megaphone and a gun, directed a chorus of these white personages, who submissively repeated texts until one of them, Dmitri Prigov, became madly uncontrollable. This rebellion marked "the birth of the hero" of contemporary Russia.

LEONID LAMM

Untitled (Washington and Lenin)
1991
acrylic on canvas
70 x 70 inches
courtesy of the Metropolitan Museum of Art, New York, anonymous gift, 1993

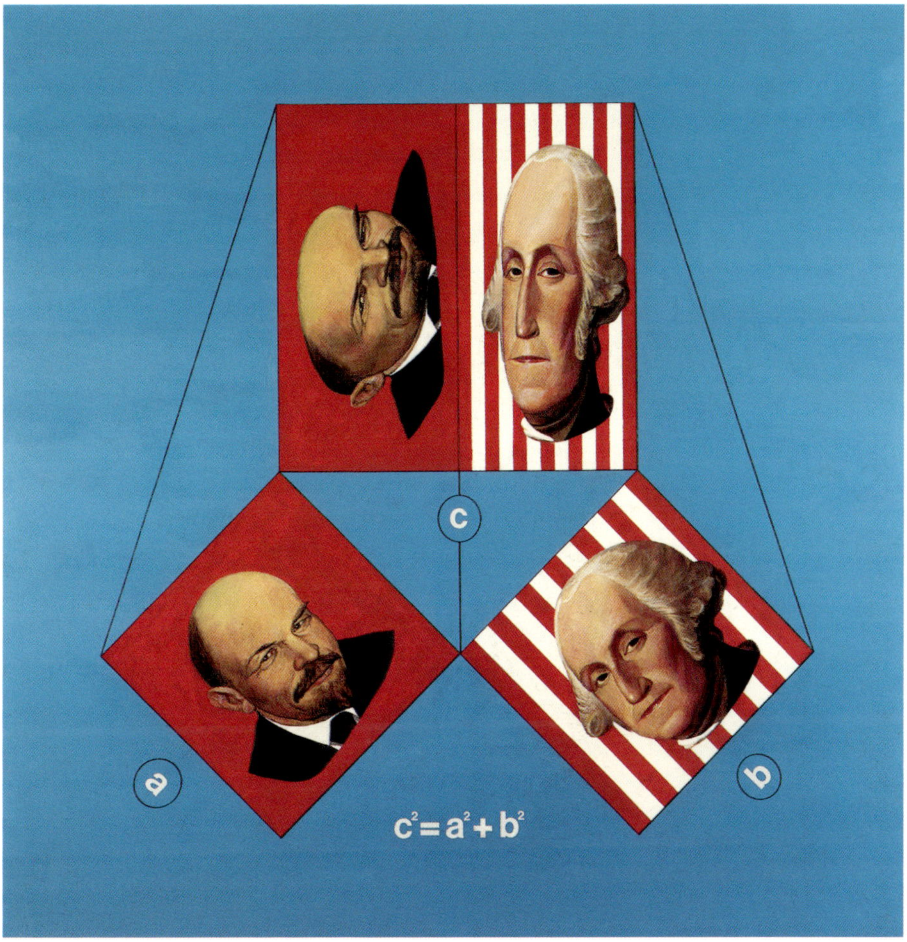

Leonid Lamm, who did not emigrate until 1982, after having spent three years in Soviet jails, was fascinated with American billboards and the manufactured look. This painting juxtaposes images of George Washington, the first American president and "father of his country," and the founder of Soviet Communism, Vladimir Ilyich Lenin, and links them with an algebraic formula that results in distorted images of both national leaders.

LEONID LAMM

Dollar
1990–93
brass, aluminum, enamel
21 x 6 x 6 inches
courtesy of the artist

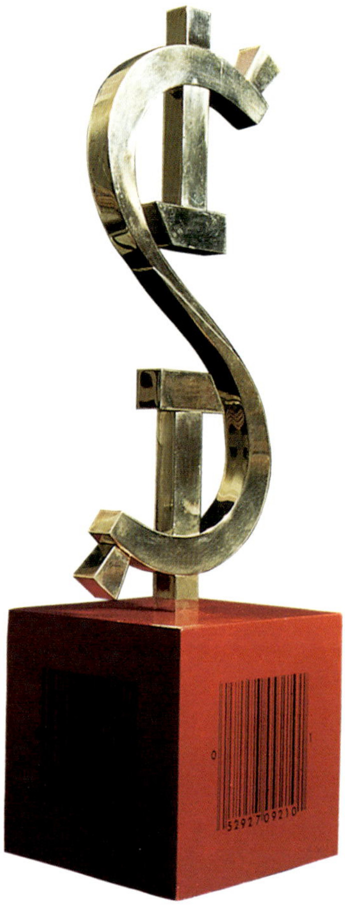

In this work, done about the time of the final collapse of the Soviet Union, Lamm cleverly combined the American dollar sign with the Soviet hammer and sickle and mounted them both on a bar code, perhaps to imply that American and Russian economies were firmly entwined, and that both now rested on the open marketplace.

BORIS ORLOV

The Battleship
n.d.
enamel on aluminum
77 x 38 x 18 inches
courtesy of Marshall Cogan,
Trace International Holdings Inc.

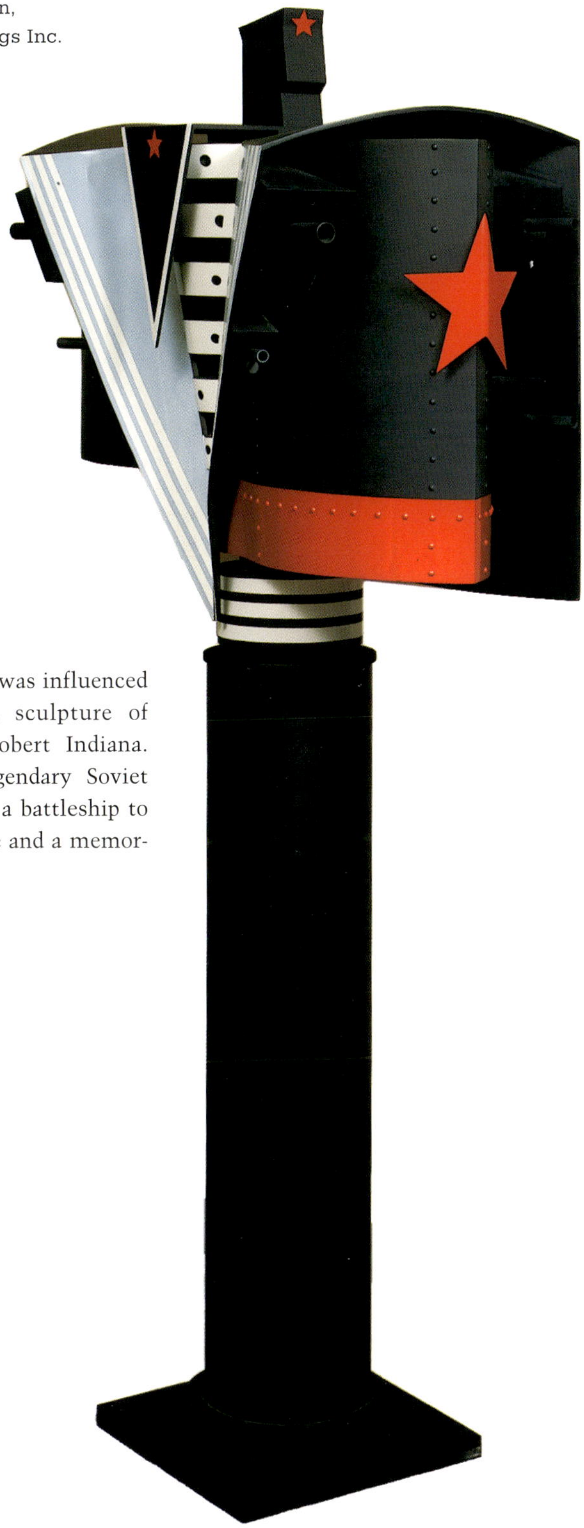

Orlov's *Battleship* series was influenced by the 1960s political sculpture of American pop artist Robert Indiana. Orlov combined the legendary Soviet sailor-hero and pieces of a battleship to make a military machine and a memorial at the same time.

ROSTISLAV LEBEDEV

Big Solitaire
1981
felt tip pen on pasteboard
4 3/4 x 3 1/8 inches (each card)
courtesy of Norton Dodge

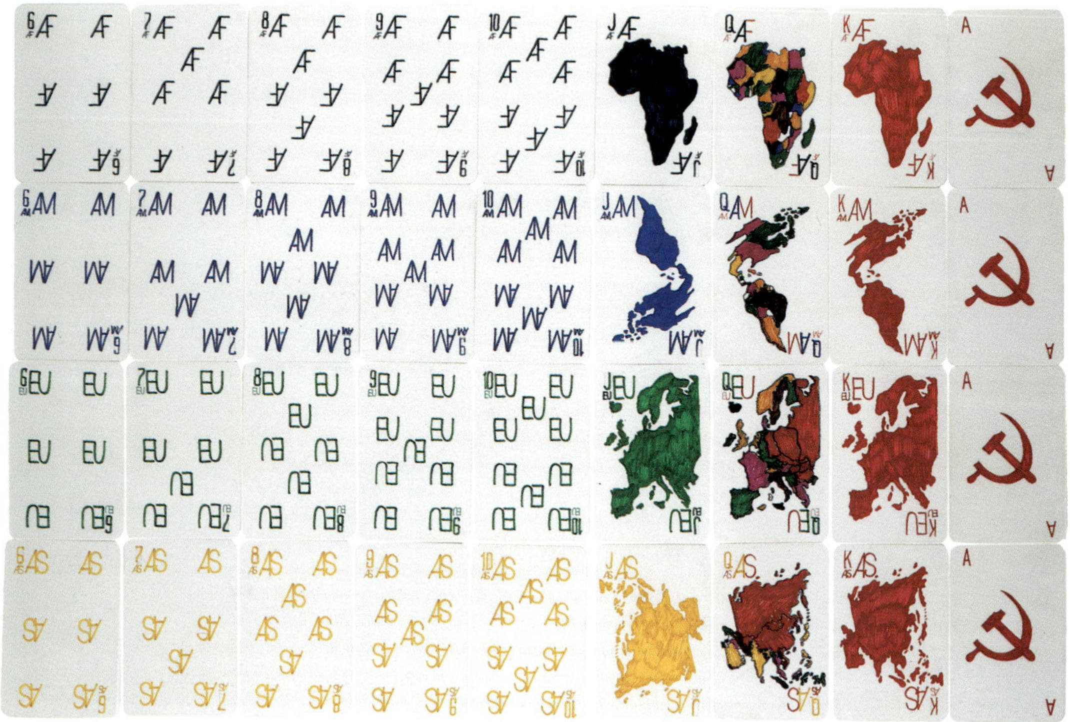

Lebedev made several sets of playing cards that represent various nations and political and economic ideologies, as if they were merely a game. One set, *Big Solitaire*, shows each continent on the earth becoming more and more red, as Communism conquers more and more of the world.

In the other one, *Souvenir Cards*, the red cards, which in an ordinary deck would be hearts and diamonds, are transformed into the Soviet hammer and sickle and a *matryoshka* (nesting folk art doll). The matryoshka suit includes important symbols of Russian culture—the balalaika folk instrument is the jack, the birch forest is queen, the vodka bottle, ironically, is king, and the doll, the number one folk souvenir from Russia, is the ace. Representing the hammer and sickle are Communist flags and slogans.

The black cards, clubs and spades, are represented by a dollar sign and a Coke bottle. In the Coke, "consumerist," suit, are the automobile as jack, a sex symbol as queen, a "cowboy" sporting two Coke bottles as pistols, and Coca-Cola, America's number one cultural export to the world, as the ace. The "dollar" suit includes words and symbols of democracy and capitalism.

Souvenir Cards
1986
4 x 2 1/2 inches (each card)
felt tip pen on pasteboard
courtesy of Norton Dodge

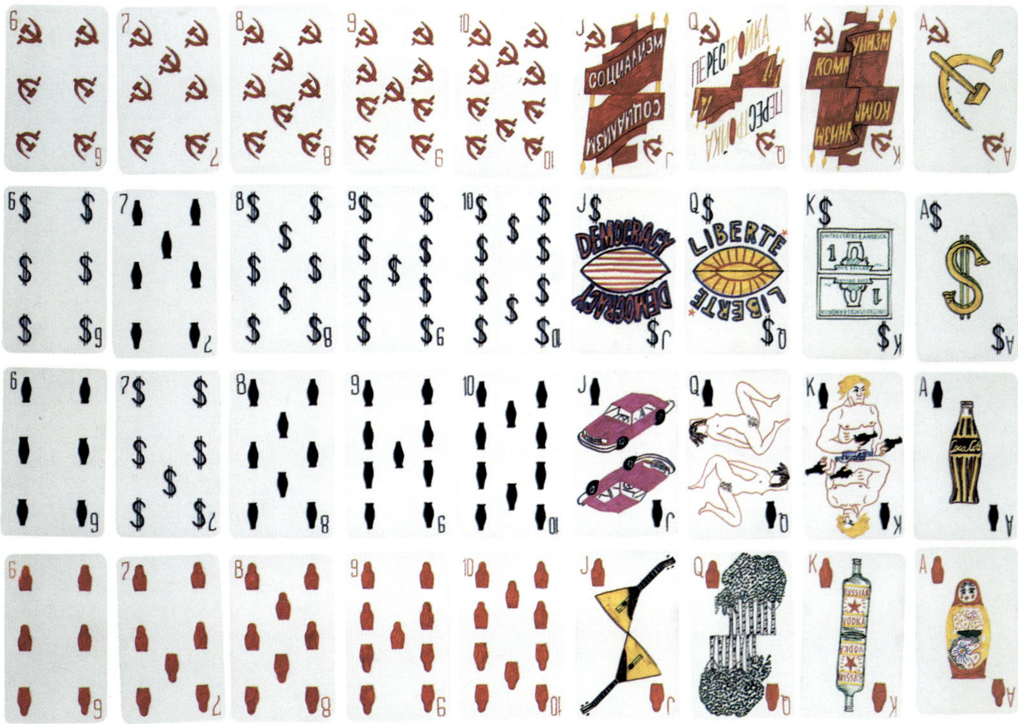

GRISHA BRUSHKIN

Logies, Part I
1987
oil on linen
92 x 153 1/2 inches, 35 panels total, each panel 18 1/2 x 22 inches
courtesy of Marshall Cogan, Trace International Holdings Inc.

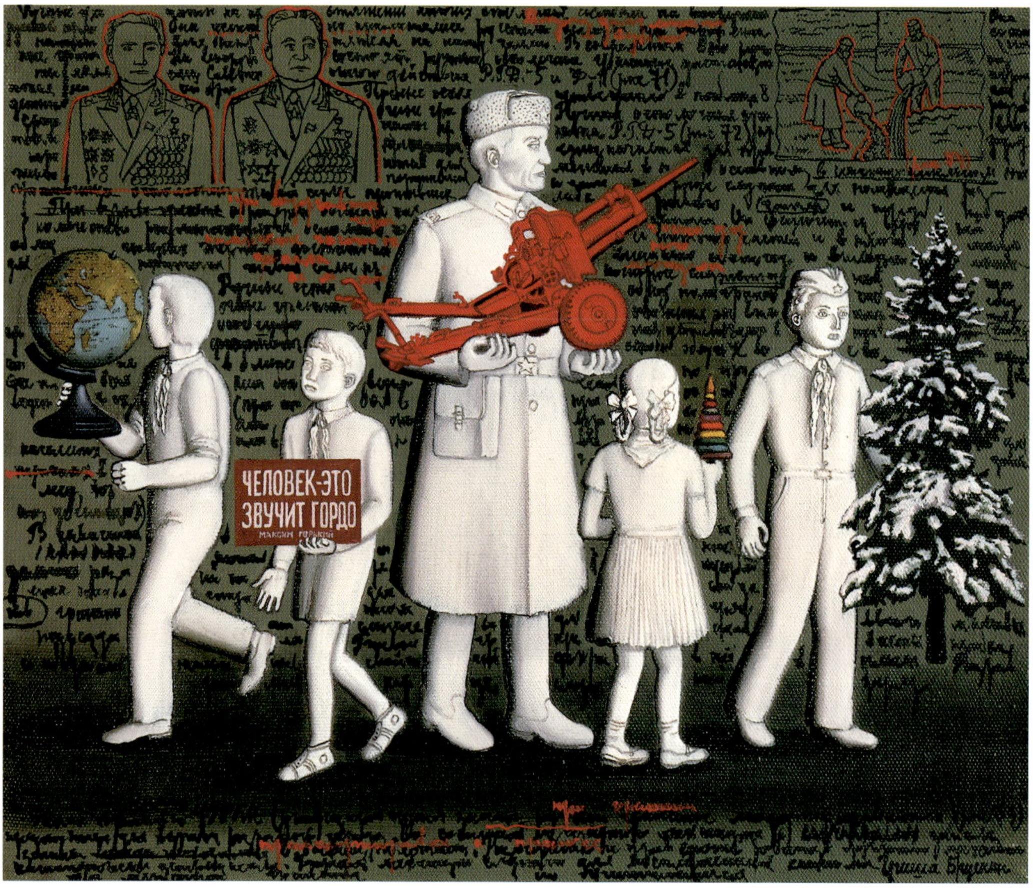

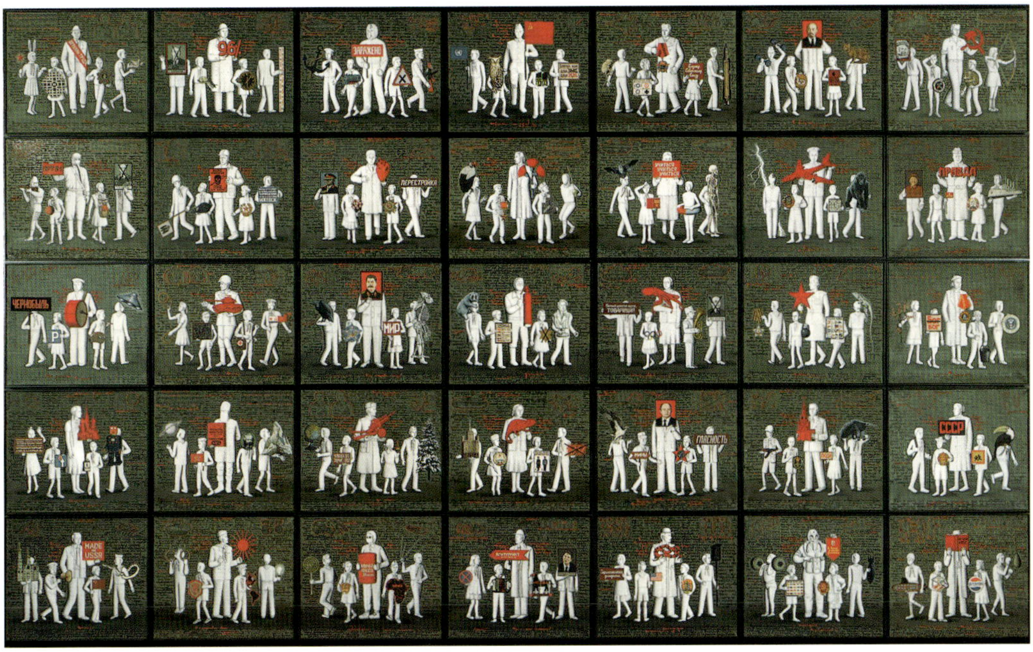

Bruskin's small Moscow studio required that he make this large work from many smaller paintings. This one includes 35 small panels and is part of his *Book of Life*, his collection of Soviet archetypes. Bruskin's quasi-scientific catalogue of Soviet officialdom classifies them by profession and social station. It mocks the strict hierarchy that existed in the "classless society" that was a goal of Communist ideology. The white figures that represent the classified officials are based on cheap plaster statues. Bruskin's classifications also include mythological figures and beasts, and references to the Bible.

The title, *Logies I*, refers to the suffix that denotes areas of learning, such as biology or psychology. Without the root word, a "logy" has no meaning or function, no base in reality. The bloated bureaucracy of the Soviet system is the "logy" in Bruskin's painting.

GRISHA BRUSHIN

Birth of a Hero, Figure G — Borderguard with Marker
1989 (from the series *Birth of the Hero*)
ed. 6/8
painted bronze and aluminum
16 1/2 x 7 3/8 x 3 inches
courtesy of Marlborough Gallery, New York

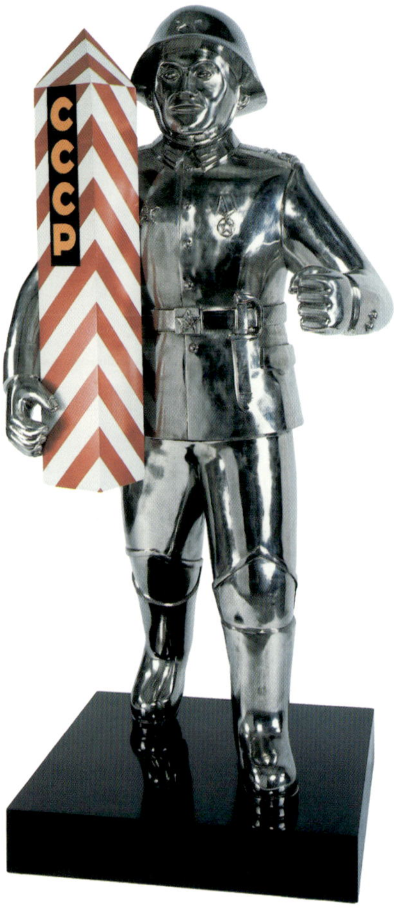

Borderguard with Marker, made from a cheap-looking shiny metal that implies garden-variety propaganda sculptures, represents the imperialist policies of the Soviet Union that were developed during the era of dictator Joseph Stalin, who controlled the Soviet Union from 1924 to 1953. The soldier is shown moving the troublesome bordermarker, which stood in the way of Communist goals. Imperialism is still a driving force for many of the nationalists in Russia today.

opposite page

Vassiliev's "Monuments" series was marked by a sensitive perception of the broken chain of history in Russia. This work, done during the chaos that preceded the fall of the Soviet Union in 1991, shows a familiar statue of Vladimir Ilyich Lenin, founder of the Soviet Union and sometimes called the most important figure of the twentieth century, in the midst of a prophetic golden sunset, framed by jarring white abstract forms. Vassiliev's deep perspectival view of Lenin's monument serves as a last glimpse of an object that sinks into oblivion, evoking a kind of sadness and desolation—an emotion that recalls the plays of nineteenth-century Russian author Anton Chekov.

OLEG VASSILIEV

Before the Sunset
1990 (from the series *Monuments*)
oil on canvas
82 1/2 x 65 inches
courtesy of the Phyllis Kind Gallery, New York

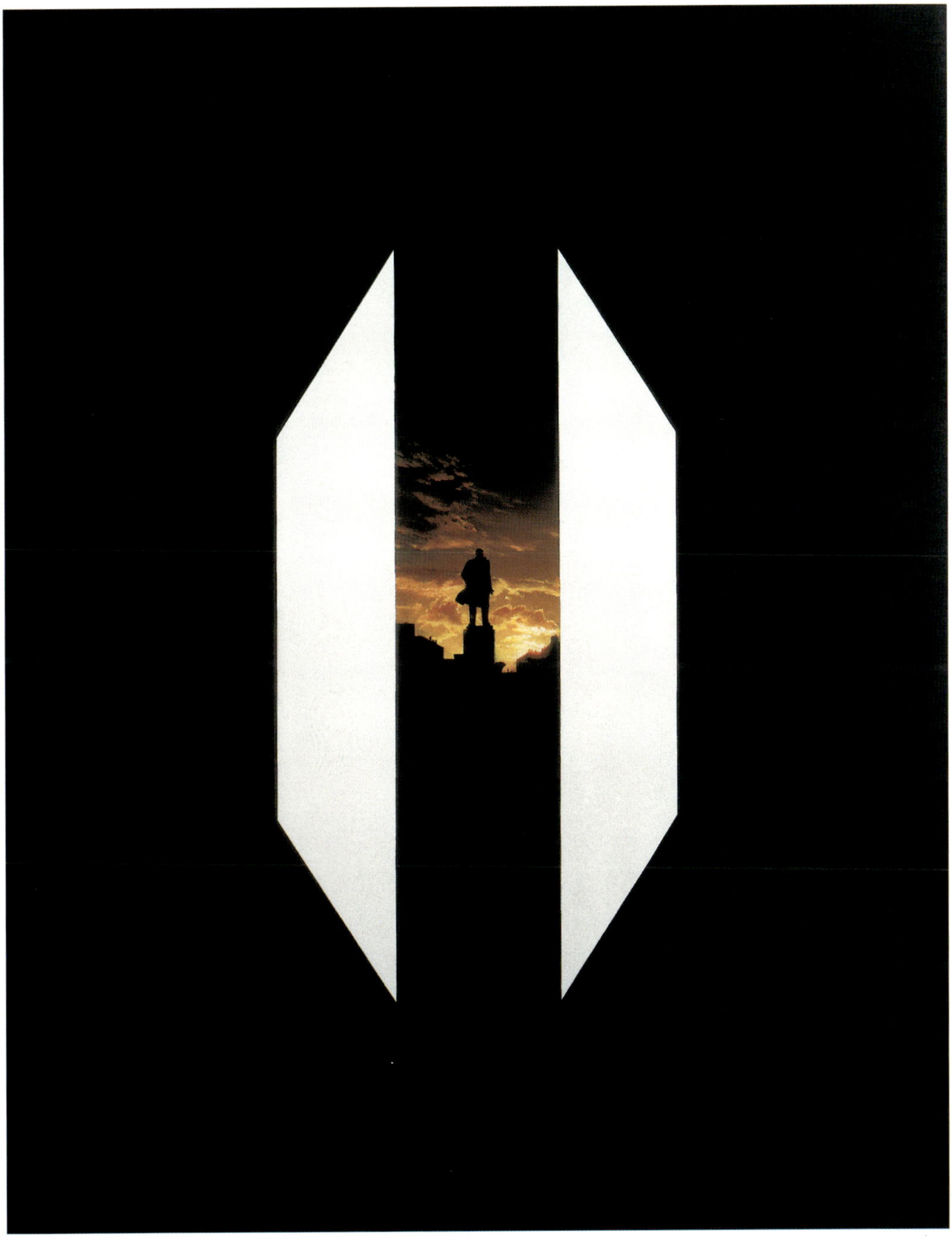

3 POST-SOVIET

PERESTROIKA, A PROGRAM OF ECONOMIC AND POLITICAL RESTRUCTURING IN THE SOVIET UNION LAUNCHED BY MIKHAIL GORBACHEV IN 1985, AND THE SUBSEQUENT COLLAPSE OF THE SOVIET UNION UNDER BORIS YELTSIN IN 1991, PROVOKED A NEW WAVE OF SOTS ART. POST-SOVIET SOTS ART CAN BE DIVIDED INTO TWO MAIN STREAMS: LOW-CULTURE, EVEN KITSCH, OBJECTS SUCH AS FOLK TOYS THAT MOCK SOVIET LEADERS, AND A KIND OF HISTORICAL NOSTALGIA THAT OCCURRED WHEN RUSSIAN ARTISTS PERCEIVED THEY WERE WITNESSING ONE OF THE GREATEST EVENTS OF THIS CENTURY.

SOTS ART

The exploration of Russian history and myth, national ambitions and reality, new changes and old distortions, and the relationship between the East and the West, sharpened the focus of sots art. The end of censorship in Russia meant that sots artists were no longer underground and that even émigré artists were able to bring their ideas back to Moscow. In post-Communist Russia, ideology continues to be part of the essential fabric of Russian life, but nationalism and religion have replaced Communism as the source.

In 1992, **Komar and Melamid**, who were by then well known in both the East and West, created a project they called *Monumental Propaganda.* The artists proposed that instead of destroying Soviet monuments, their meaning and purpose should be changed to fit the new order. For example, Lenin's Mausoleum, long an accepted and necessary part of Soviet life and Communist ideology, should contain constantly changing advertising messages rather than Lenin's preserved body. Young artists have continued to use the irony of sots art to examine the rapid, and often destructive, changes that they see around them every day. Begun as a part of a mischievous underground, sots art in post-Soviet Russia has taken on new life.

Komar and Melamid ironically presented the leader of the Russian revolution, Vladimir Ilyich Lenin, as a bronze statue, arm outstretched in a pose well known from Soviet propaganda paintings and sculpture. The symbols of American capitalism—New York City's Chrysler building (topped by a Soviet red star) and the ubiquitous golden arches of McDonald's—surround him. Instead of pointing the way toward a glorious future under Communism, the outstretched arm of the greatest Russian leader of the twentieth century has been reduced to hailing a cab in the center of the world that vanquished his ideals.

VITALY KOMAR AND ALEXANDER MELAMID

Lenin Hails a Cab
1993
oil on canvas
48 x 36 inches
courtesy of the Sloane Gallery of Art, Denver

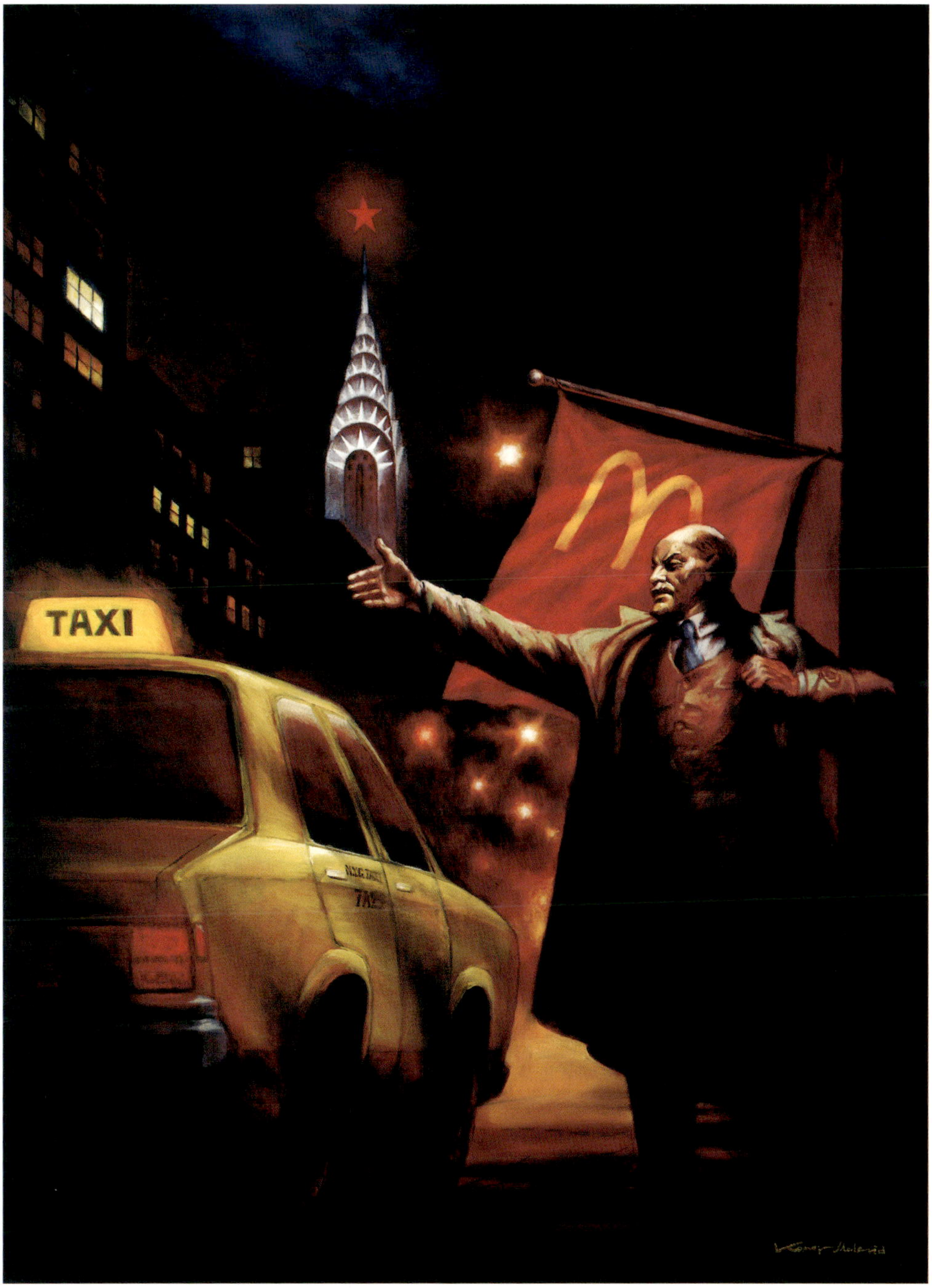

VITALY KOMAR AND ALEXANDER MELAMID

Monumental Propaganda
1991–93
four hand-colored computer graphics
11 x 7 inches
courtesy of the artists

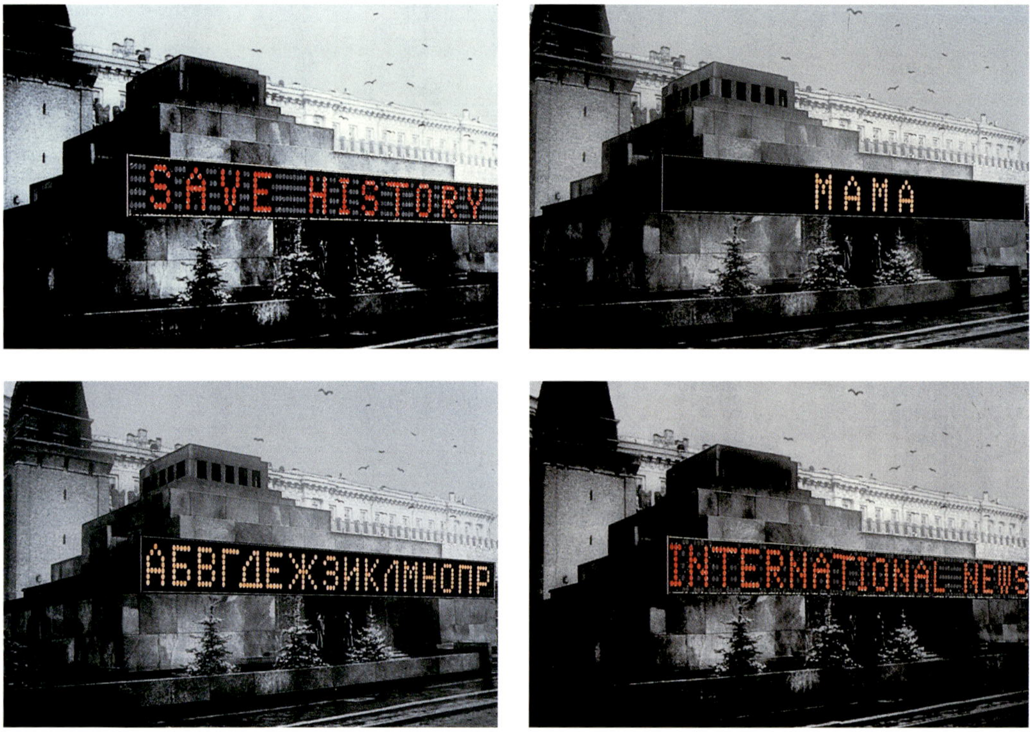

After the final collapse of the Soviet Union in 1991, Komar and Melamid, by now world-recognized artists, proposed that the new government not rush to destroy the monuments of the old Soviet Union. The artists suggested that, instead, the preserved body of the founder of the Soviet Union, Vladimir Ilyich Lenin, on display in a mausoleum in Moscow since his death in 1924, and long the subject of reverence—and joking—be replaced with LED (light emitting diode) advertising messages and words and letters running in a continuous stream across the monument. This replacement would let the world know that the old heroes of Communist ideology and their didactic slogans were finally dead, replaced by the brash new technology propaganda of capitalism. The inclusion of such irrelevant words as "mama" or letters of the alphabet serves to occasionally dissolve all political meaning and make the installation into pure conceptual playfulness.

ALEXANDER KOSOLAPOV

Have You Eaten Caviar Lately?
1996
mixed media installation
courtesy of the artist

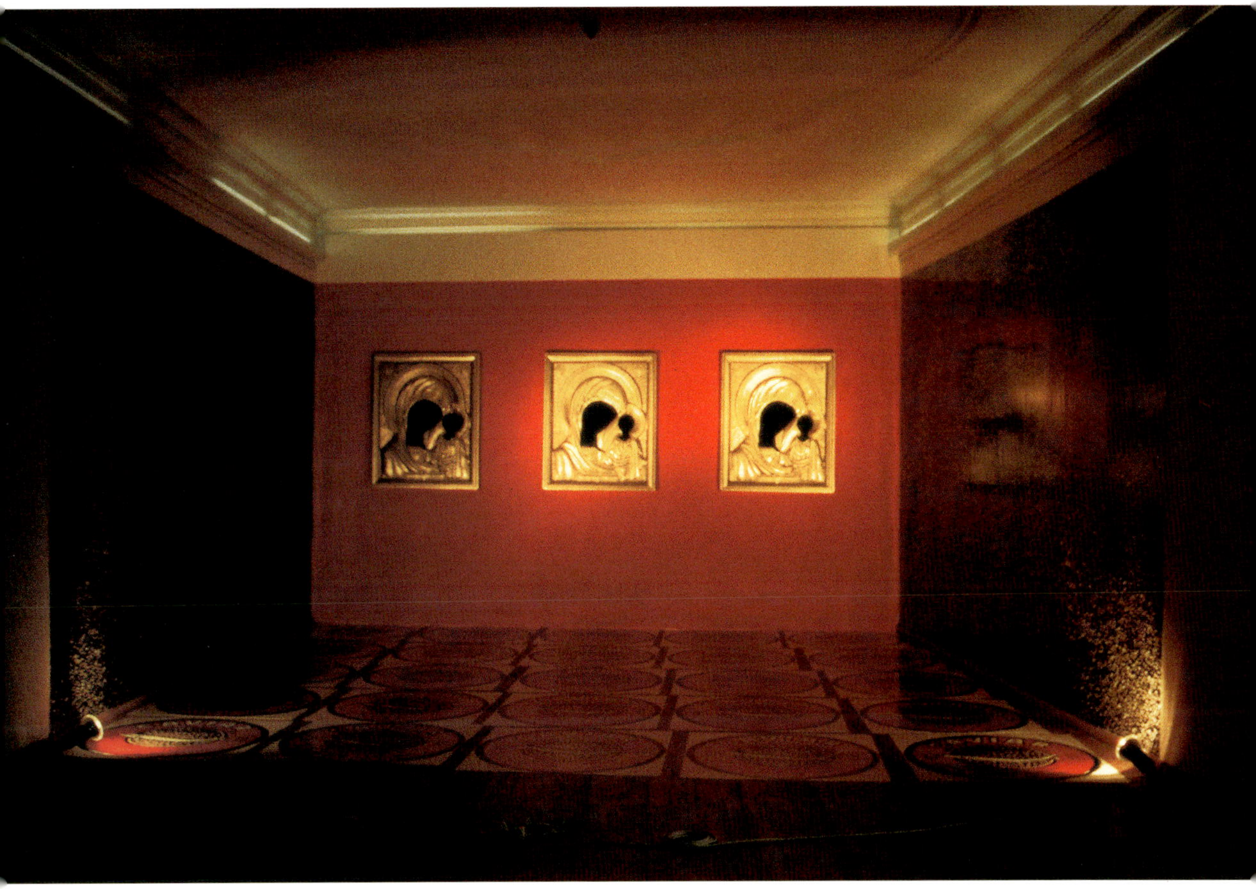

Alexander Kosolapov's installation, *Have You Eaten Caviar Lately?*, spoofed the replacement of Communist ideology with religious and consumerist dogma. He subverted the American advertising slogan "Have you driven a Ford lately?"—the easily accessible Ford car helped equalize people—to describe a product, caviar, that symbolizes privilege. By combining caviar with traditional Russian religious images, Kosolapov explored ideas about the power and privilege of the new Russian state and its affiliation with the authoritarianism of the Russian Orthodox church.

OLEG VASSILIEV

Freedom is Freedom
1995 (from the series *Monuments*)
oil on canvas
48 x 40 inches
courtesy of the Sloane Gallery of Art, Denver

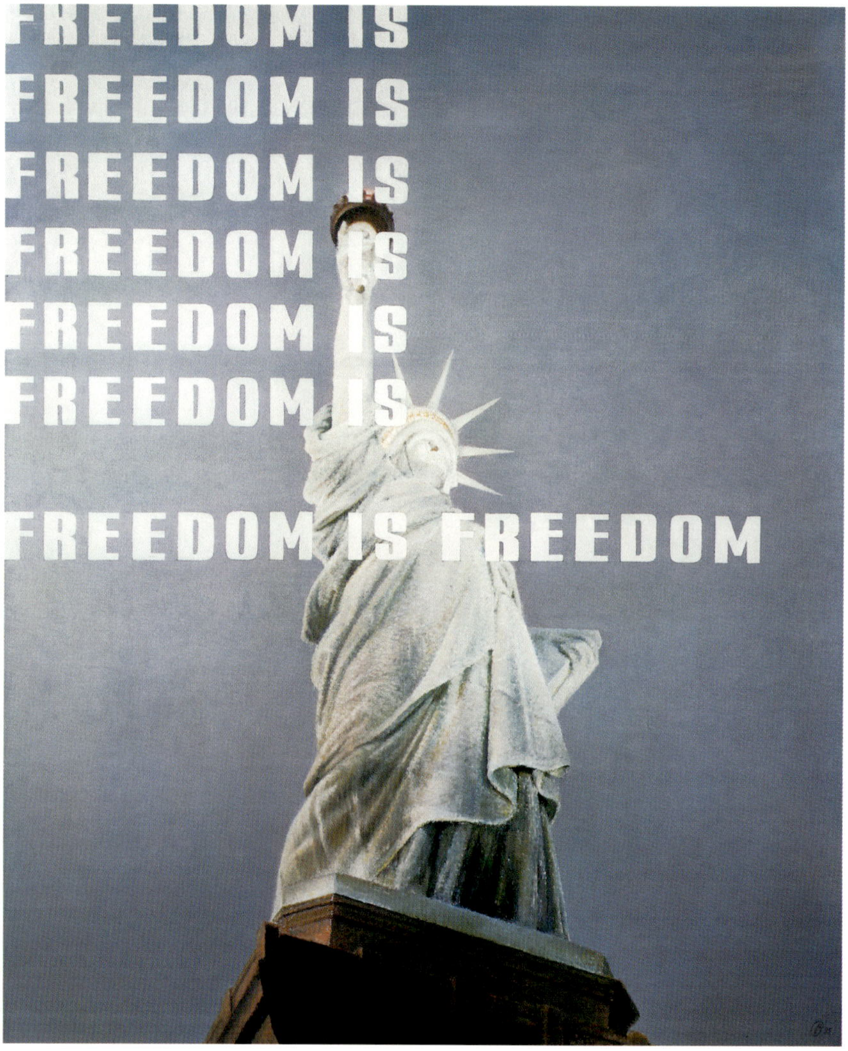

Vassiliev, who depicted Lenin's monument against the setting sun, here shows the symbol of America, the Statue of Liberty, in clear daylight. The repetition of the words "Freedom is" and the conclusion that "Freedom is Freedom" may have a double meaning. Freedom, represented to the émigré artist by the Statue of Liberty, is so basic that it is indefinable. But it may refer to the idea that for many émigré artists, freedom became a hollow achievement because the forces that controlled the art market in the Western world were not necessarily more benign than Soviet censorship.

NICOLA OVCHINNIKOV

Russian Order
1989
mixed media
43 5/16 x 13 x 3 15/16 inches
courtesy of the artist

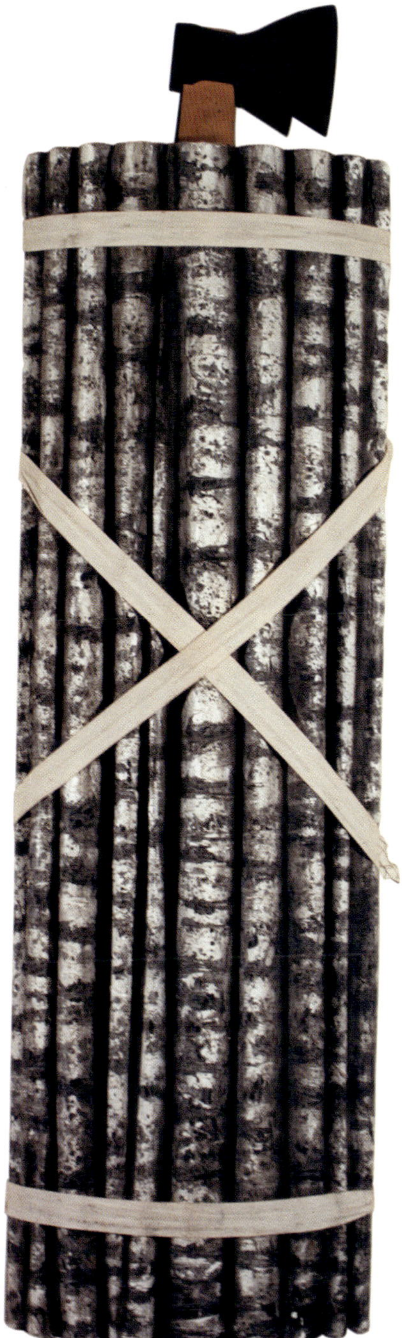

Nicola Ovchinnikov, a young Moscow artist, changes old signs and banners into new symbols. For *Russian Order*, he combined birch logs—from the Russian birch forest celebrated by poets and painters—with the traditional Russian ax to form a new fasces, originally a symbol of official authority in ancient Rome. Benito Mussolini's Fascist Party of Italy was named for the fasces, and an emblem similar to Ovchinnikov's *Russian Order* was the Italian Fascist Party's official emblem.

ROSTISLAV LEBEDEV

The Landscape of the Caucasus
1996
acrylic on canvas
39 3/8 x 78 3/4 inches
courtesy of the artist

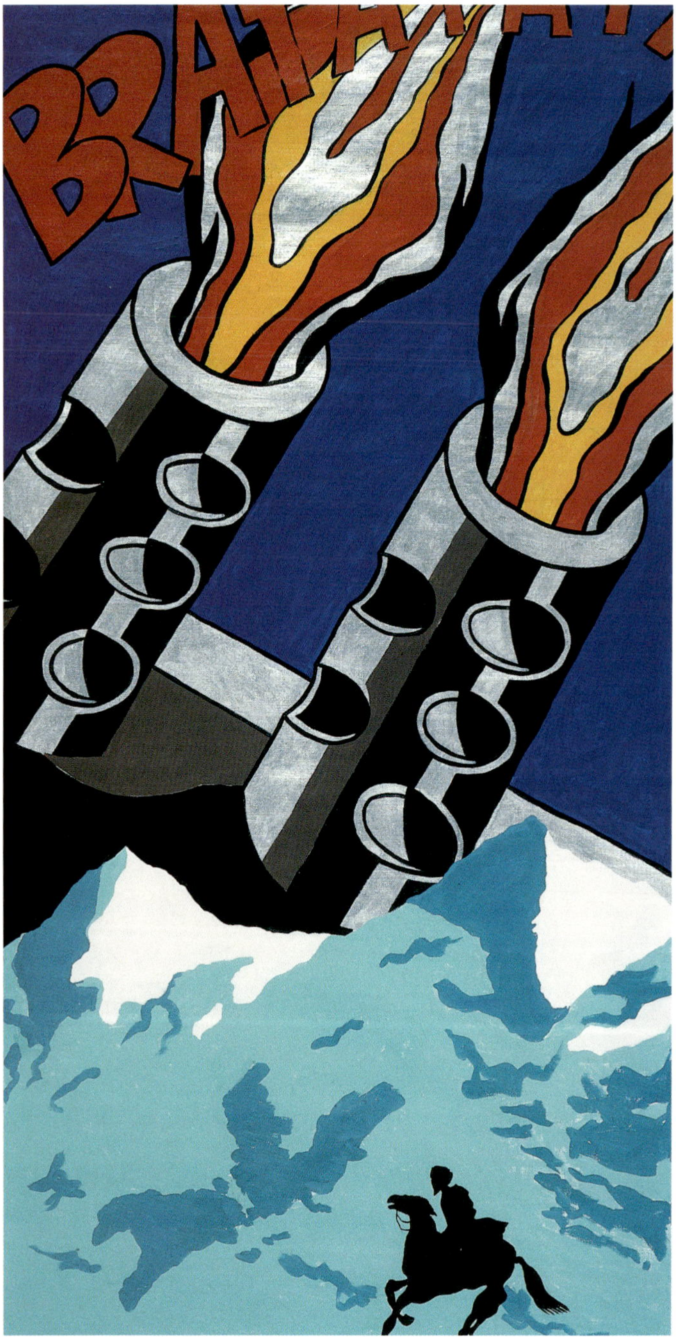

In Lebedev's painting a wild Caucasus horseman, from the package of the Kazbek cigarette brand, is silhouetted against Mount Kazbek, one of the highest mountains in the Caucasus range of the far eastern region of Russia. Above this scene loom giant, fire-spitting gun barrels and the cartoon-like onomatopoetic words for gunfire. The painting is inspired by American pop artist Roy Lichtenstein's *As I Opened Fire,* which includes similar images.

Kazbek cigarettes were Joseph Stalin's preferred smoke. Stalin was born in Georgia, in the Caucasus region. The combination of the Caucasus scene and the firing guns refers to the bloody Chechnya war, which began in 1994 when the Russian army was sent to quell the rebellion precipitated by the 1991 declaration of independence by the republic of Chechnya, north of the Caucasus mountains. The tough mountain people were a match for the demoralized Russian army and thousands of civilians died in Chechnya before the Russians finally drove the last remaining Chechen defenders out of the capital, Grozny, in 1995. The Chechen war was covered widely by the Russian media, which had only recently been freed from extensive government censorship.

AFRIKA [SERGEI BUGAEV]

Anufriev Goes Reconnoitering, Anti-Lissitzky Green
1990
oil on canvas
40 x 59 inches
courtesy of the I-20 Gallery, New York

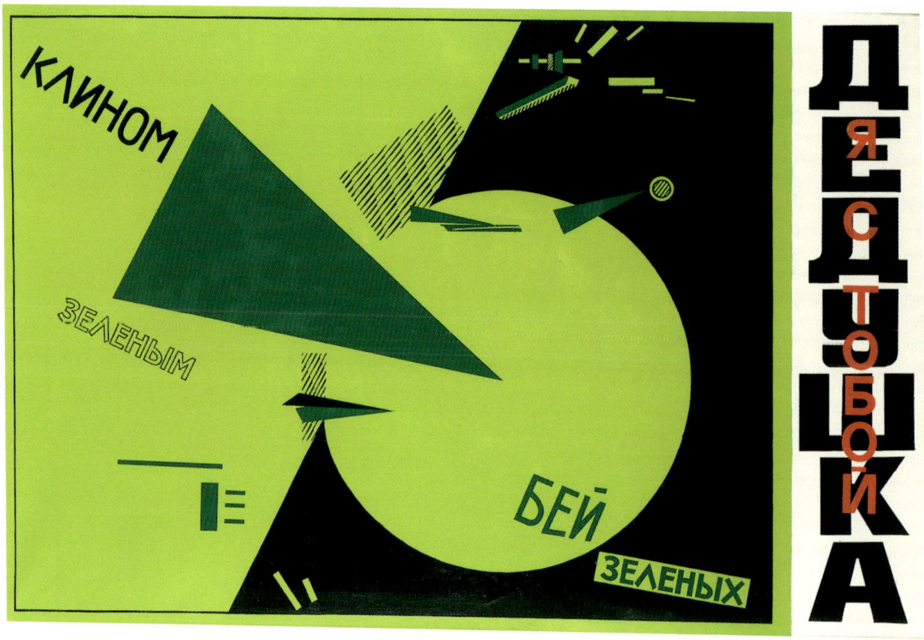

St. Petersburg artist Sergei Bugaev, who goes by the artistic moniker of Afrika, painted *Anti-Lissitzky Green* as a parody of a famous work by El Lissitzky, a member of the suprematist art movement begun by Kazimir Malevich in the 1910s. Suprematism's geometric abstraction was in favor during the early years of the revolution but was later suppressed when officials decided that abstract art did not help meet the goals of the Soviet state. The geometric abstraction of the revolutionary period came to represent the avant garde—the "official" style of non-official artists during the 1950s and 60s.

El Lissitzky's 1920 work, *Beat the Whites with the Red Wedge,* referred not only to the forms of the painting, where a red wedge penetrated a white circle, but also to the opposing forces of the Russian Revolution of 1917, the Communist "red" army and the tsarist "white" forces. By changing the value-laden colors red and white to different shades of green, and putting the word "grandpa" on the side, Bugaev destroyed both the aesthetics of the suprematist avant-garde and the revolutionary meaning of El Lissitzky's work, and declared both aesthetics and meaning to be old-fashioned.

NATASHA TURNOVA

The Heroes of the Civil War
1991
oil on cardboard
left figure: 48 1/2 x 34 5/8 inches
center figures: 48 1/2 x 57 1/2 inches
right figure: 55 1/8 x 35 3/4 inches
courtesy of the artist

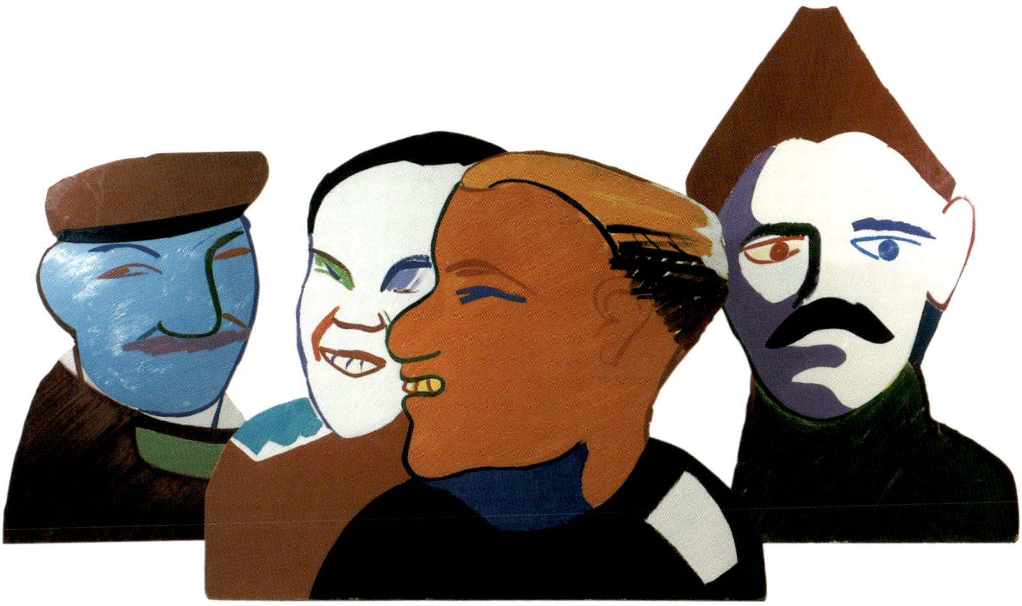

After *glasnost*, a policy of openness launched by Mikhail Gorbachev in 1985, Soviet history began to be revealed as mythology and, in some cases, fantasy. Turnova represented these heroes of the civil war as bold young conquerors but with a hint of the demonic. As predicted by the Russian writer Fyodor Dostoyevsky in his 1871–72 novel, *The Demons* or *The Possessed*, these heroes were joined by bloody deeds that ultimately made them criminals. The childlike style with which Turnova presented these military hero-criminals underlines the contradictions of Soviet history-mythology.

Mikhail Frunze, one of the fathers of the Soviet Red Army, is represented on the left. After frequent arrests for revolutionary activity between 1905 and 1915, Frunze became one of the outstanding Red Army commanders of the civil war. He later established a system of training that emphasized ideology and that the main task of the Soviet Army was to promote world revolution under the banner of Communism.

The hero on the far right is Semyon Budenny, who joined the Imperial Russian Army in 1903. He later took part in the revolution that overthrew the imperial government and played a crucial role in the Soviet Red Army victory over the White, antirevolutionary forces. He was named a "Hero of the Soviet Union" in 1958 but later fell from favor.

TENGIZ

The Big Three
1991
acrylic on canvas
18 x 15 inches
courtesy of the Sloane Gallery of Art, Denver

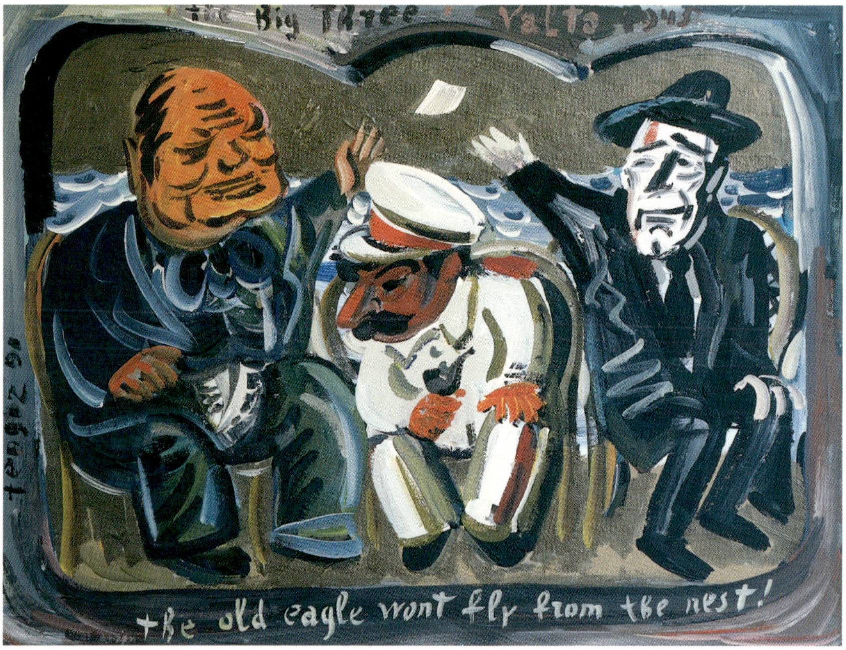

Tengiz spoofs the "big three" leaders, the American Franklin Roosevelt, British Winston Churchill, and the Soviet Union's Joseph Stalin, who planned how to divide up Europe after their alliance defeated Hitler in World War II, at a famous conference at Yalta, in the Crimea. The painting is based on an incident Churchill recorded in his memoir. According to the memoir, Roosevelt passed a note to Churchill alerting him that his fly was open. Churchill colored, tore the note to pieces, and sent a reply to Roosevelt. Stalin misunderstood this exchange as a conspiracy against the Soviet Union and instructed his intelligence agents to retrieve the torn pieces of the note and reconstruct the messages. They found only two words, "eagle" and "nest." Stalin used these two words as a code title for the conspiracy he believed Roosevelt and Churchill were plotting against him. Churchill's memoir, published after Stalin's death, explained that his reply to Roosevelt had told him not to worry because "the old eagle won't fly from its nest!"

TENGIZ

Comrade Stalin is the Best Friend of the Soviet Soccer Players!
1991–93
assemblage
courtesy of the Sloane Gallery of Art, Denver

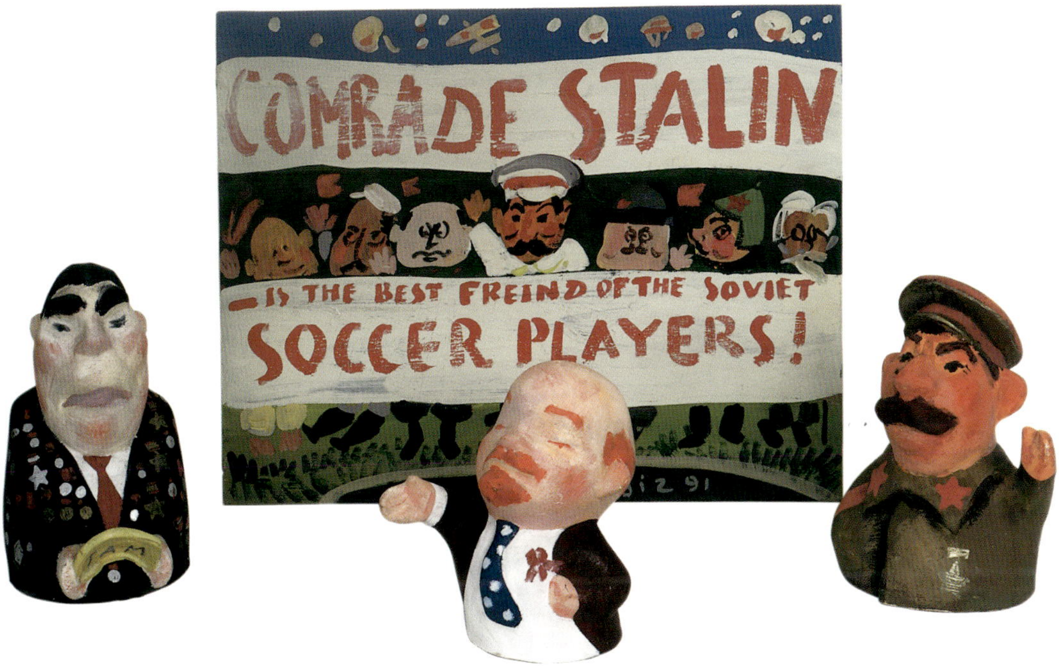

These rough figures of Vladimir Ilyich Lenin, Joseph Stalin, and Leonid Brezhnev, all repressive leaders of the Soviet Union, resemble *matryoshka* (nesting doll) folk toys. Lenin and Stalin are declaiming while Brezhnev seems to be reading from a book—the rule book? The slogan spoofs the system of official training and support that made Soviet athletes winners of many international competitions.

IRINA DANILOVA

Underwear
1996
mixed media
32 x 32 inches
courtesy of the artist

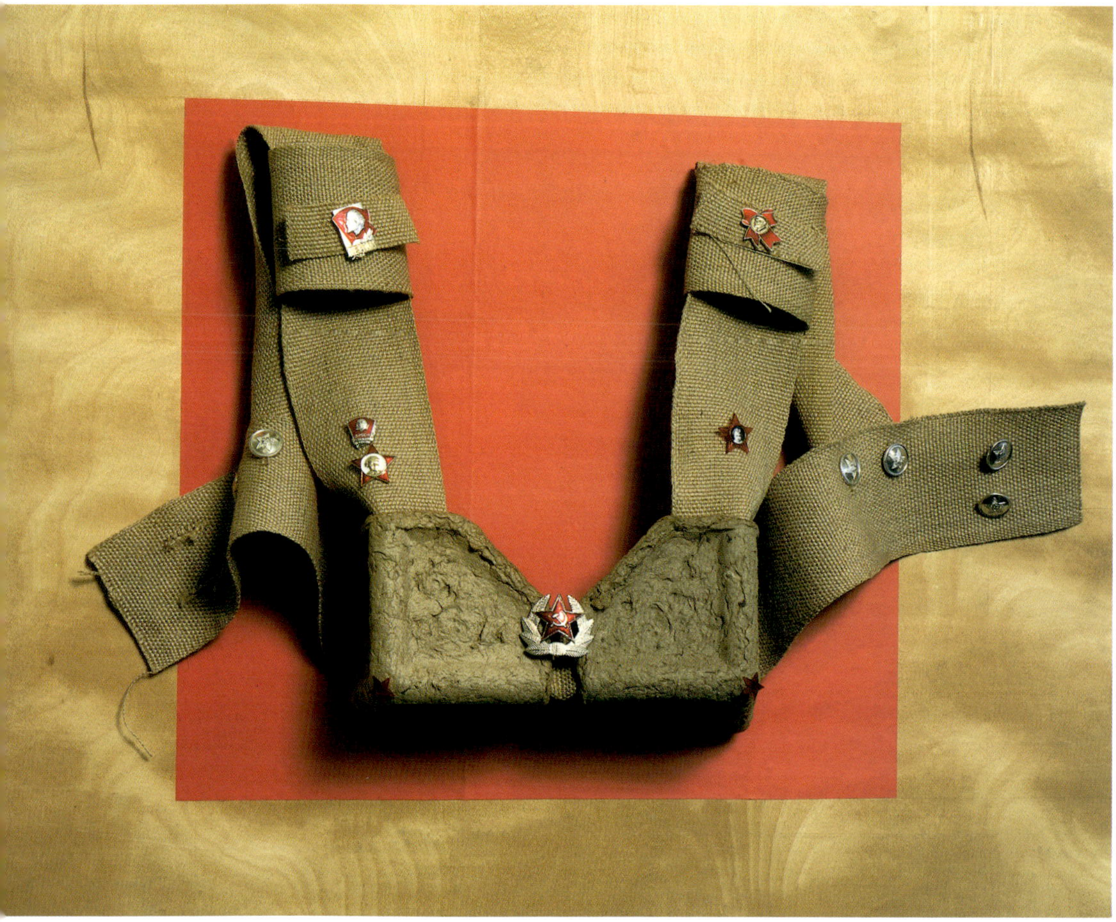

Danilova fashioned a formidable brassiere festooned with red stars and medals. It comments in a wry fashion on the equality of the sexes in the Soviet Union that allowed women the "privilege" of hard labor and negated their femininity.

GENIA CHEF

The Third Rome
1994
oil on pressed wood
9 3/4 x 12 3/4 inches
courtesy of the artist

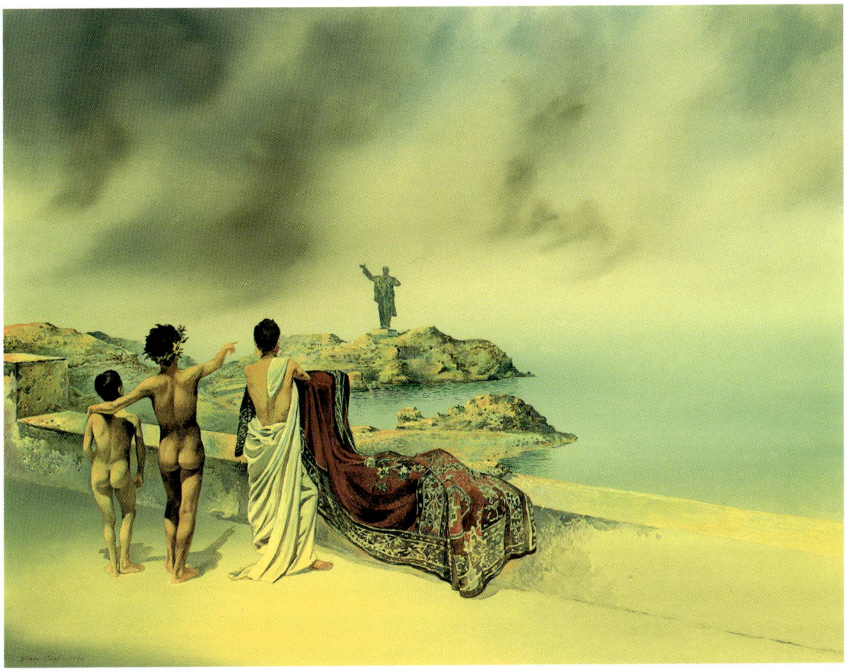

The "first" Rome became the original capital of Christianity when the Roman emperor Constantine converted to Christianity in 312 AD. In 330 he founded Constantinople (Istanbul in present-day Turkey) as the "second" Rome, the new capital of the eastern half of the Roman empire. A sixteenth-century document written by a Russian monk proclaimed that with the fall of Constantinople to the Ottoman (Muslim) Turks in 1453, Moscow had become the "third (and last) Rome," the only remaining true Christian state. The title of the Russian king, "tsar," was taken from the Roman "Caesar." The Third Rome doctrine was used to justify Russian imperial ambitions and to legitimize the idea that it was Russia's destiny to rule the world—even by the non-Christian Soviet Union.

The Third Rome depicts three "Roman" citizens pointing and staring to a far-off statue wearing a toga, whose pose remarkably resembles Soviet propaganda statues of the founder of the Soviet Union, Vladimir Ilyich Lenin, as well as the poses of Roman emperors in ancient sculpture. It evokes a sense of melancholic, yet ironic, nostalgia for lost illusions.

VADIM VOINOV

Always at the Ready
1996
mixed media on board
14 1/4 x 12 x 1 1/2 inches
courtesy of Irene Goldman

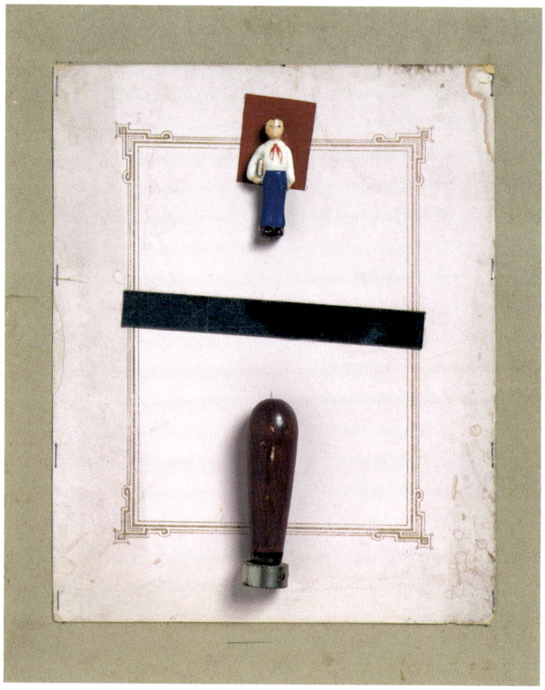

"Always at the Ready" was the motto of the Soviet Pioneers, an organization similar to the American Boy Scouts. All primary school students ultimately belonged to the Pioneers, which was started in 1920 to shape Soviet citizens from youth. The celluloid Pioneer doll and the hand stamp, which would stamp out identical messages, symbolize the aim of the Pioneer organization to mold a standard consciousness in Soviet citizens. The whole composition is mounted on a page from an old-fashioned family photo album. Behind the Pioneer doll is a red square, and below, a black rectangle. These geometric shapes refer to the principles of suprematism, Russian abstract art of the 1910s and 20s, which was briefly associated with the Communist revolutionary attempt to construct a new world.

VALERY AND NATASHA CHERKASHIN

People's Love to the People's Art
1993–94
mixed media
39 3/8 x 59 1/16 inches
courtesy of the artists

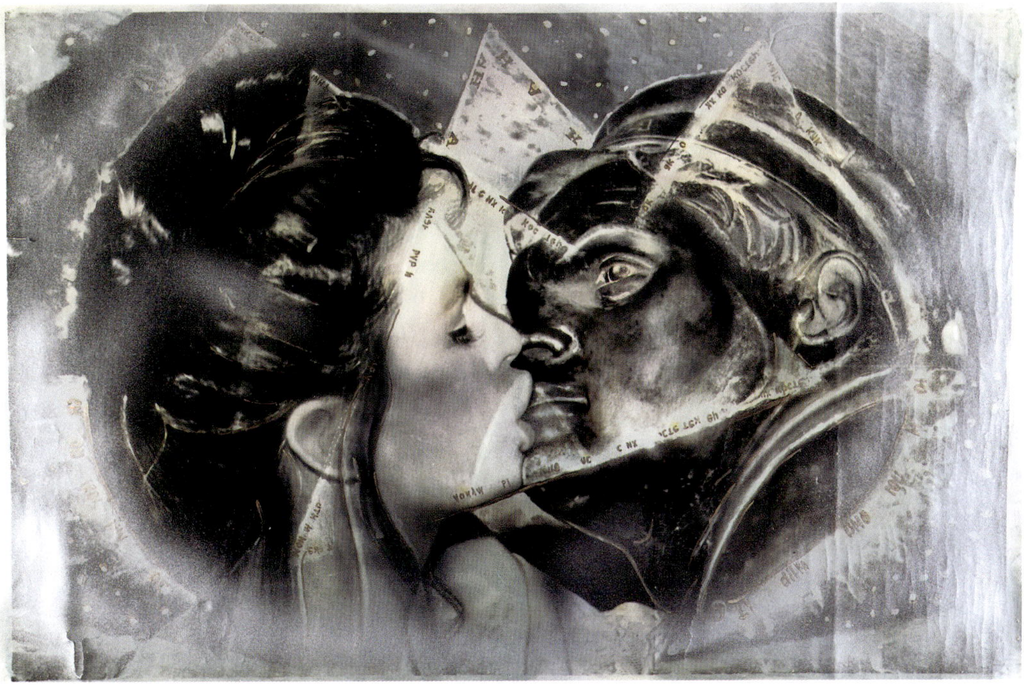

This image shows a real young woman in an erotic kiss with a typical Soviet-style sculpture. After the fall of the Soviet Union in 1991, people began to feel nostalgic about not only the old economic system, which provided a certain amount of security along with repression and absurdity, but also the "people's art," the realistic propaganda art which, though boring and predictable, abounded with images of powerful, masculine worker heroes.

VADIM GRINBERG

Soviet Playboy Number 1 (S. M. Kirov)
1989
mixed media installation
10 x 9 x 2 feet
courtesy of the artist

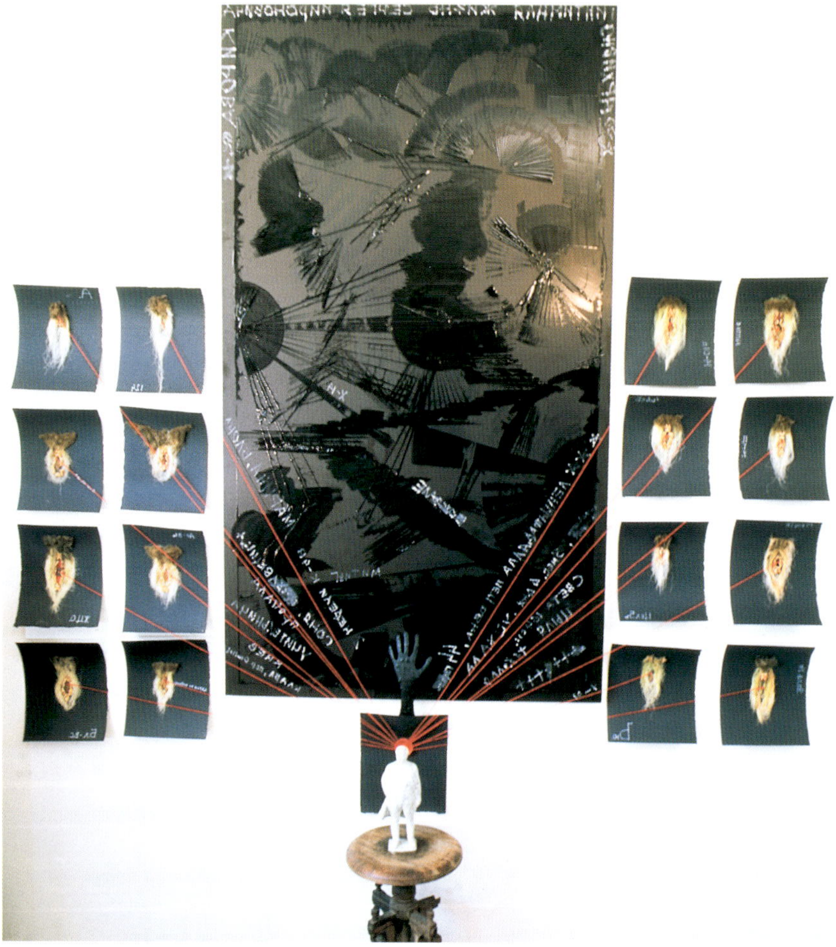

This installation was dedicated to Communist Party leader Sergey Kirov, an aggressive womanizer, who was assassinated and then canonized by Soviet dictator Joseph Stalin in the 1930s. The white figure, dwarfed by the rest of the installation, is a small, mass-produced propaganda sculpture that was painted white as part of Grinberg's collaboration with American artist George Segal, during Segal's visit to the Soviet Union in 1989. The white figure suggests Segal's trademark life-sized direct-cast white figures.

LEONID SOKOV

Watch Tower
1995
mixed media installation
17 x 5 x 5 feet
courtesy of the artist

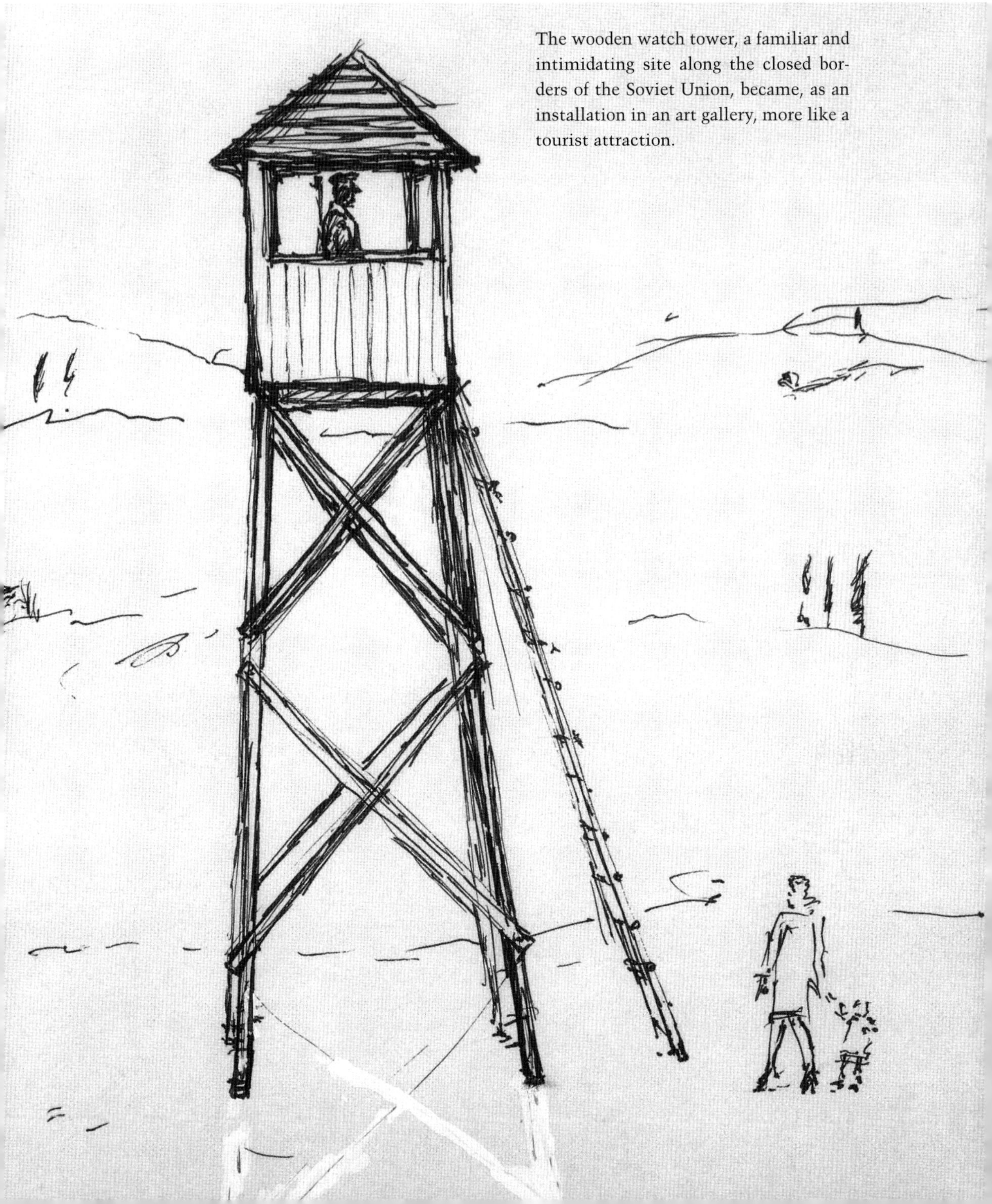

The wooden watch tower, a familiar and intimidating site along the closed borders of the Soviet Union, became, as an installation in an art gallery, more like a tourist attraction.

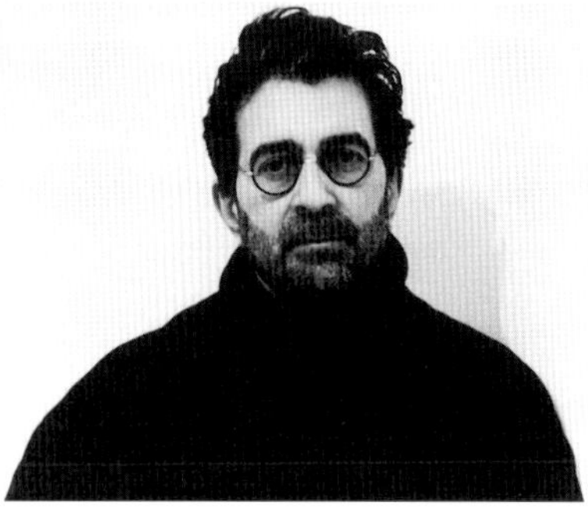

GRISHA BRUSKIN

BORN Moscow 1945

EDUCATION Moscow Textile Institute

Currently resides in New York City

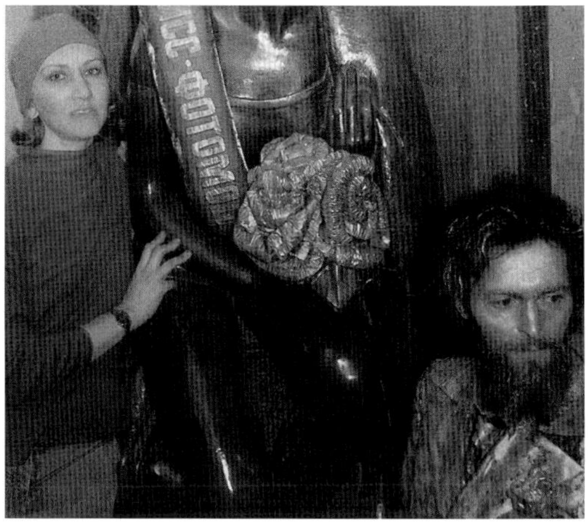

VALERY AND NATASHA CHERKASHIN

BORN Valery: Kharkov, Ukraine 1948
Natasha: Damascus, Syria 1958

Both currently live in Moscow

AFRIKA [SERGEY BUGAEV]

BORN Novorossiisk 1966

Currently lives in St. Petersburg

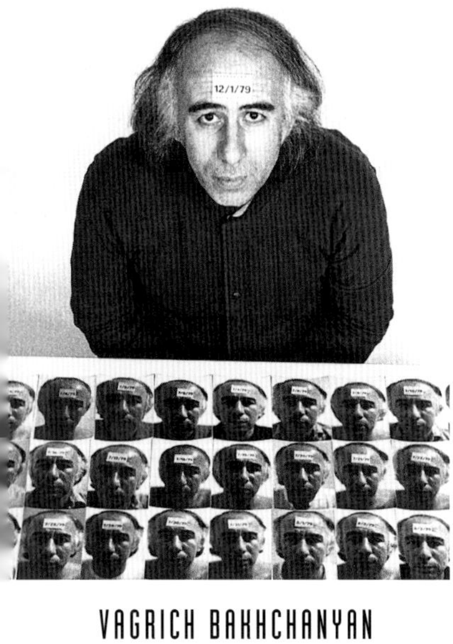

VAGRICH BAKHCHANYAN

BORN Kharkov 1938

EDUCATION 1954–57, 1960–67, Art Studio in the Palace of Culture "Metallist," Kharkov (under Russian avant-garde artists Vasily Ermilov, Alexander Kosarev, Alexei Scheglov)

Currently lives in New York

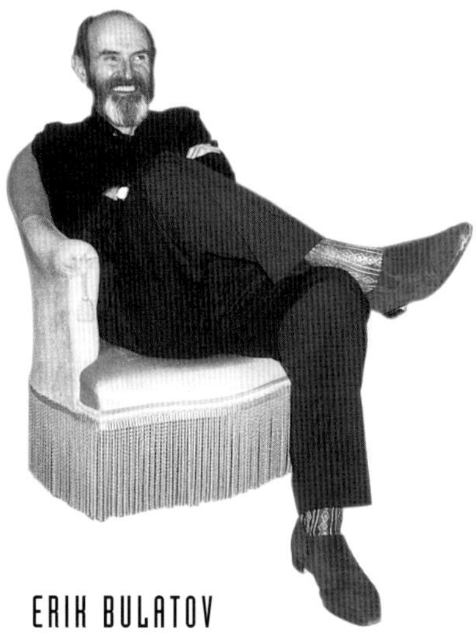

ERIK BULATOV

BORN Sverdlovsk, Ukraine 1933

EDUCATION Surikov Institute of Art, Moscow

A resident of Paris since 1991

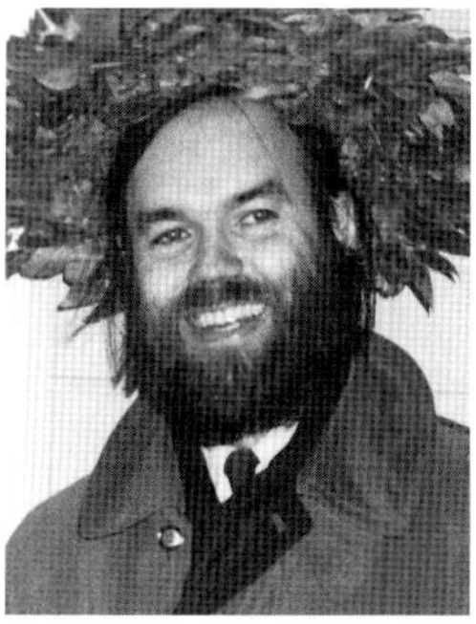

GENIA CHEF

BORN Aktjubinsk, Kazakhstan 1954
EDUCATION Moscow Polygraphic Institute
Lives in Germany and Spain

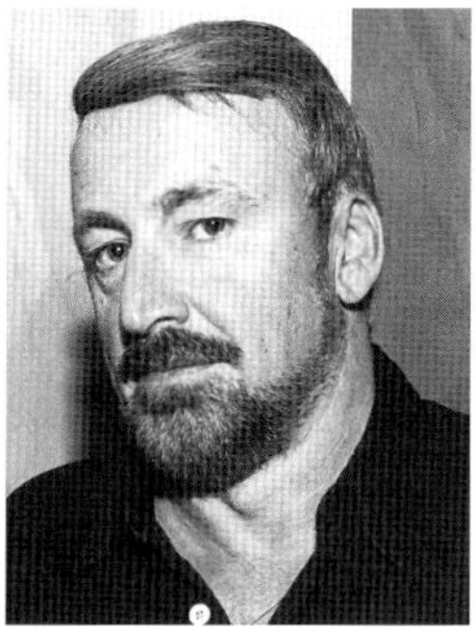

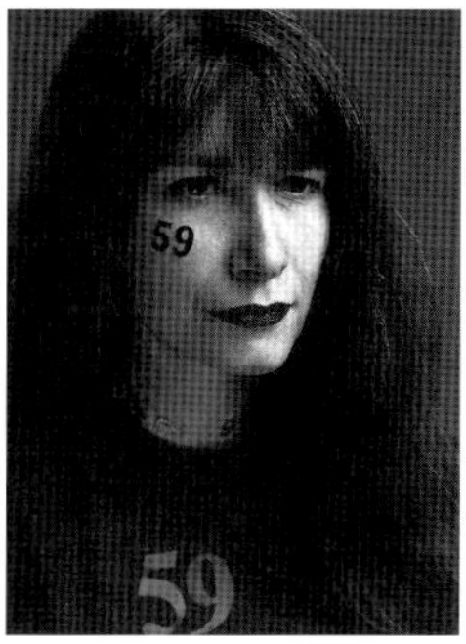

IRINA DANILOVA

BORN Kharkov, Ukraine 1959
EDUCATION School of Art and Design, Kharkov
Fine Arts College, Kharkov
School of Visual Art, New York
Currently lives in New York City

MIKHAIL CHERNISHOV

BORN Moscow 1945
EDUCATION Zagorsk Art School, Russia
Has resided in New York since 1981

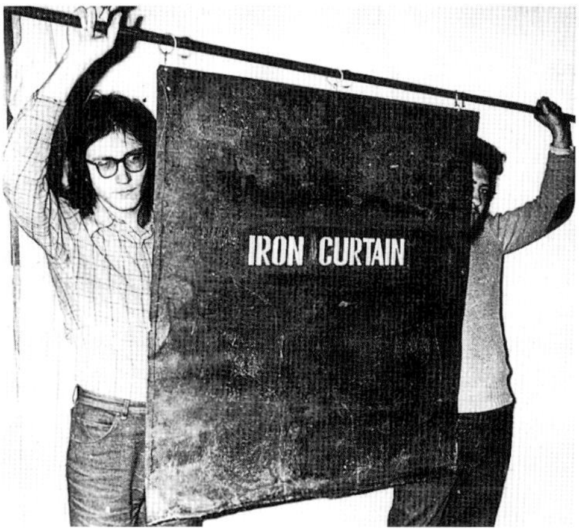

THE NEST [MIKHAIL ROSHAL-FEDOROV, GENADY DONSKOY, VICTOR SKERSIS]

GENADY DONSKOY

BORN Moscow 1956
EDUCATION Stroganov Institute, Moscow
Lives in Russia

VICTOR SKERSIS

BORN Moscow 1956
EDUCATION Stroganov Institute, Moscow
Currently lives in the U.S.

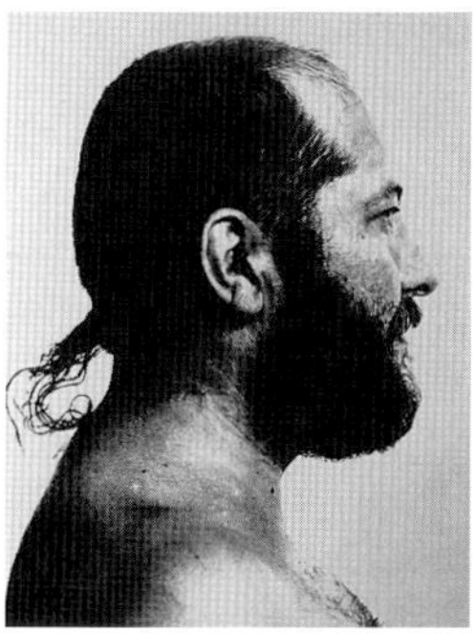

MIKHAIL ROSHAL-FEDOROV

BORN Moscow 1956
EDUCATION Moscow State Teachers Training Institute
Lives in Moscow

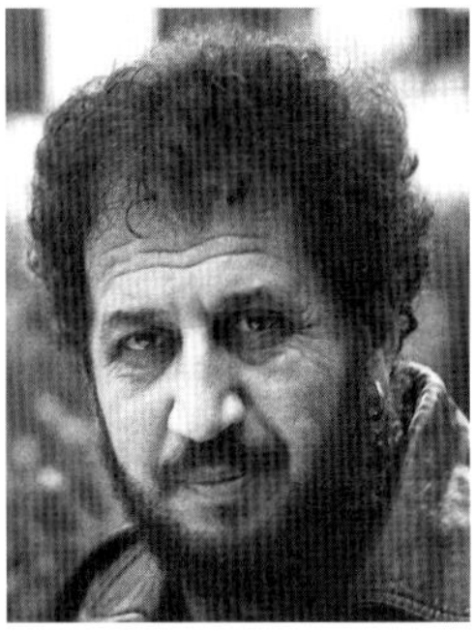

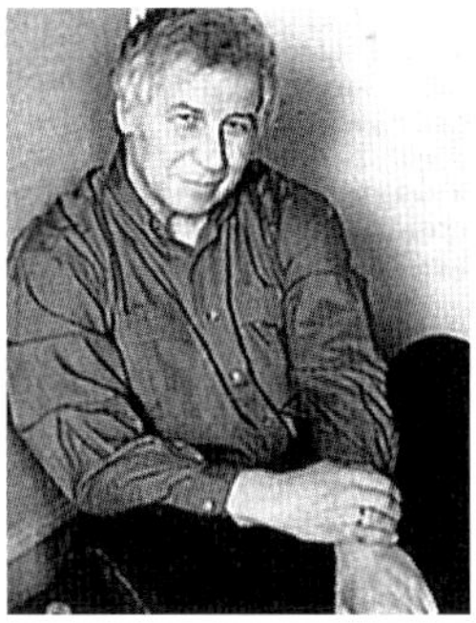

ILYA KABAKOV

BORN Dnepropetrovsk, Ukraine 1933
EDUCATION Surikov Institute of Art
Currently resides in New York

VADIM GRINBERG

BORN Odessa, Ukraine 1947
EDUCATION Pedagological University, Odessa
Currently lives in Los Angeles

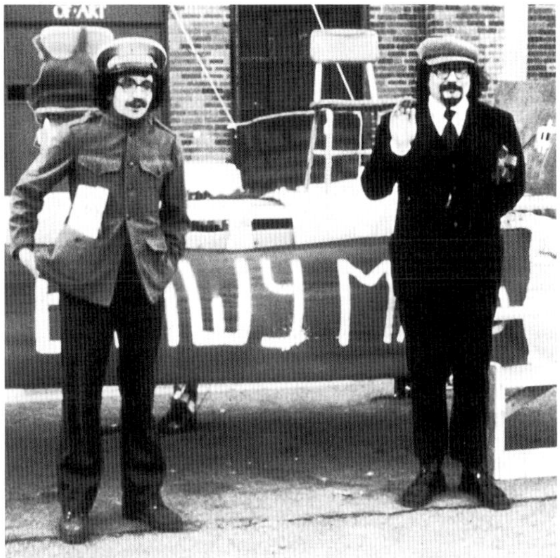

VITALY KOMAR AND ALEXANDER MELAMID

BORN Komar, Moscow 1943
Melamid, Moscow 1945
EDUCATION both at the Stroganov Institute of Art, Moscow
Both currently live in New York

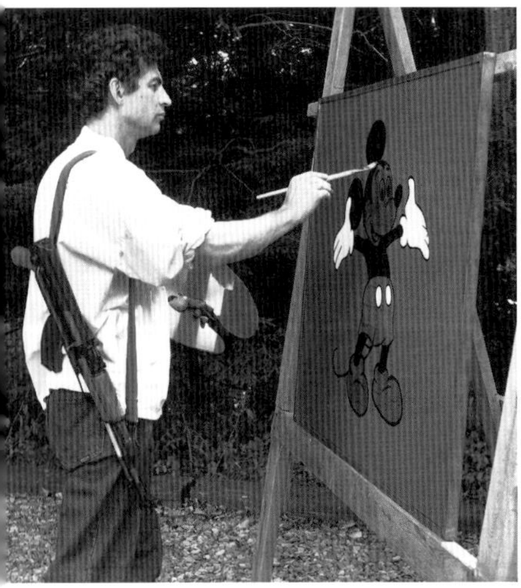

ALEXANDER KOSOLAPOV

BORN Moscow 1943
EDUCATION Stroganov Institute of Art, Moscow
Currently lives in New York

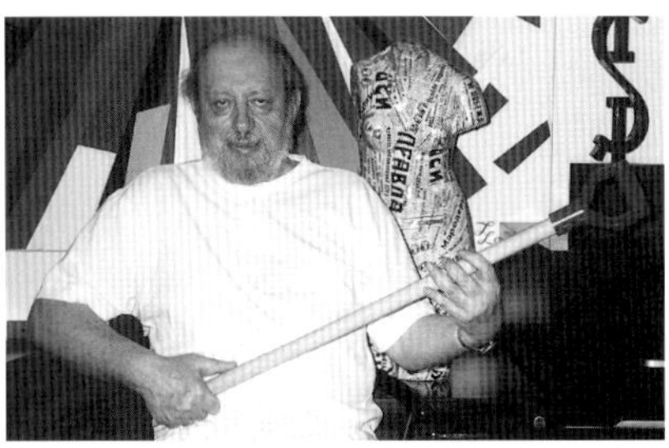

LEONID LAMM

BORN Moscow 1928
EDUCATION Moscow Institute of Architecture
Moscow Polygraphic Institute
Resident of New York since 1982

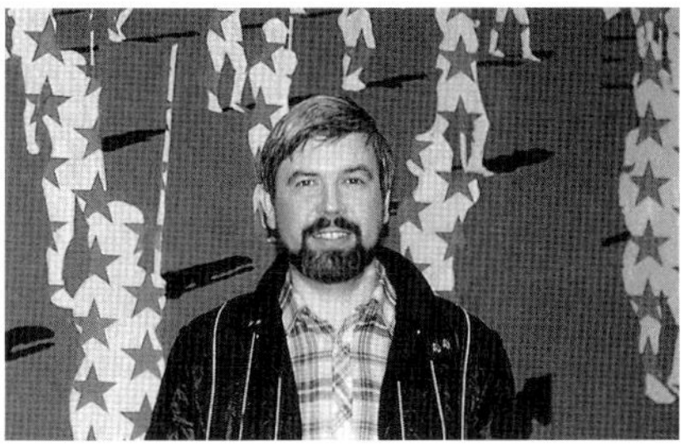

ROSTISLAV LEBEDEV

BORN Moscow 1946
EDUCATION Pedagological Institute Art Department
Lives in Moscow

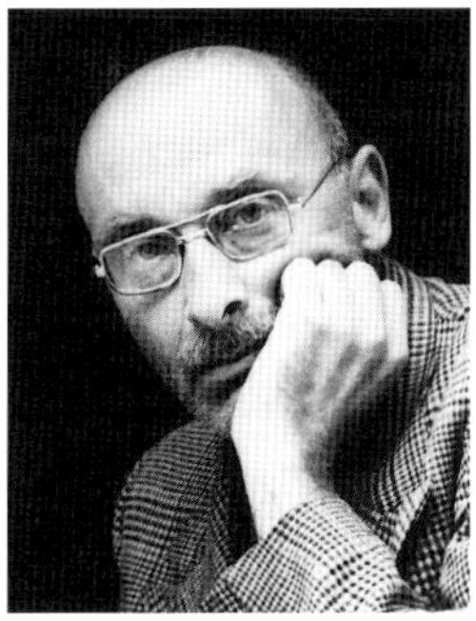

OSCAR RABIN

BORN Moscow 1928
EDUCATION Academy of Arts, Riga
Currently lives in Paris

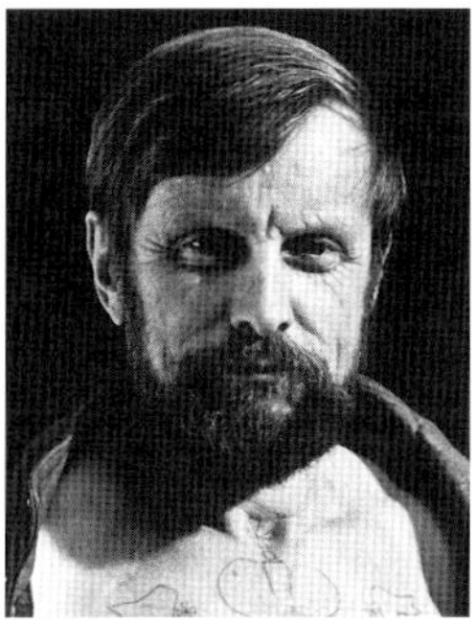

BORIS ORLOV

BORN Moscow 1941
EDUCATION Stroganov Institute of Art, Moscow
Currently lives in Moscow

MIKHAIL ROGINSKY

BORN Moscow 1931
EDUCATION Art School "In Memory of 1905," Moscow
Currently lives in Paris

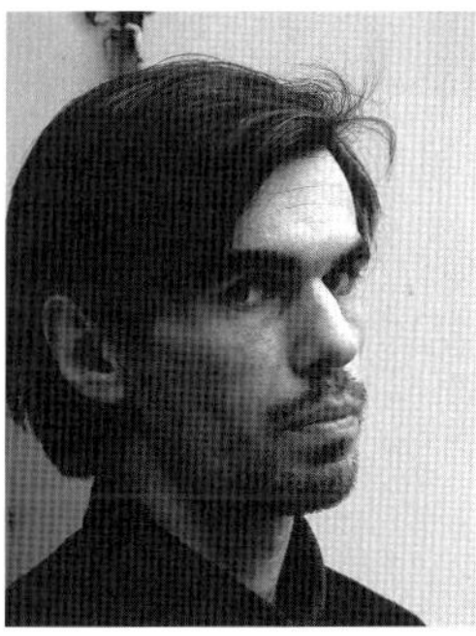

NICOLAS OVCHINNIKOV

BORN Moscow 1958
EDUCATION Art School "In Memory of 1905," Moscow
Lives in Moscow

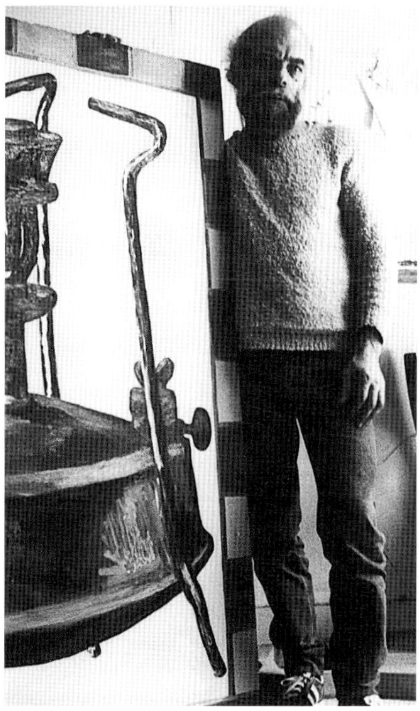

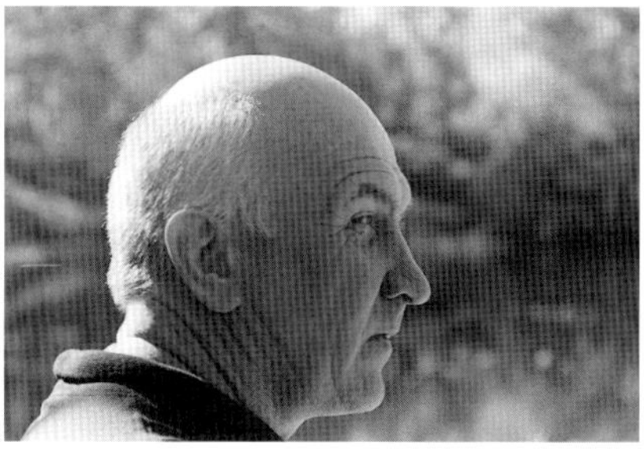

LEONID SOKOV

BORN Kalinin, Russia 1941
EDUCATION Stroganov Institute
Currently lives in New York

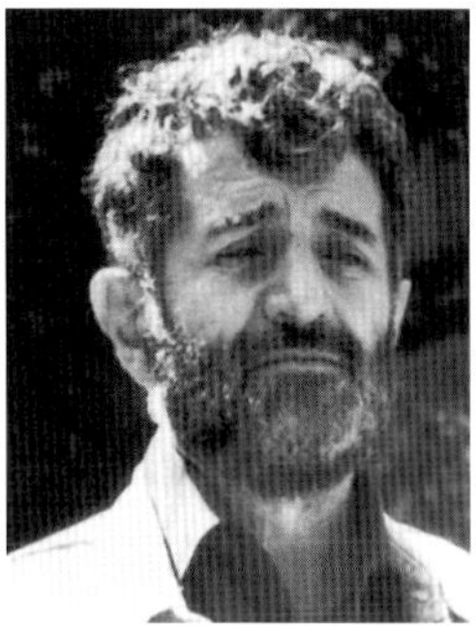

TENGIZ [TENGIS MIRZASHVILI]

BORN Mestia, Georgia 1934
EDUCATION Georgian Art Academy
Lives in Tbilisi, Georgia

NATALIA TURNOVA

BORN Kabul, Afghanistan 1957
EDUCATION Moscow School of Design
Lives in Moscow

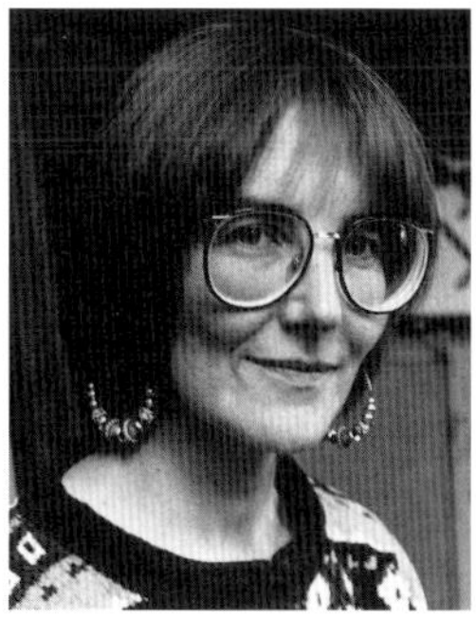

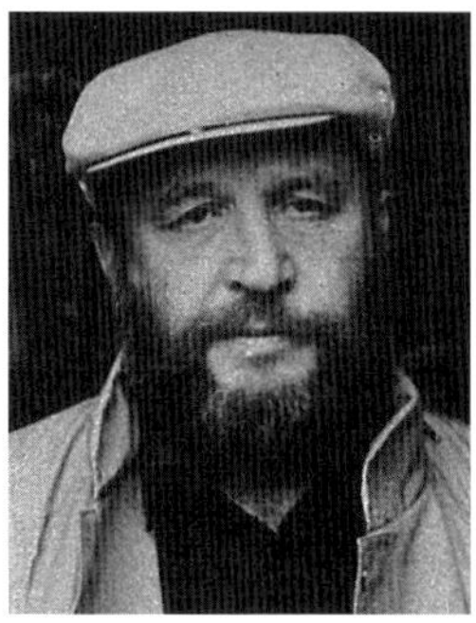

VADIM VOINOV

BORN Leningrad 1940
EDUCATION Leningrad University
Lives in St. Petersburg

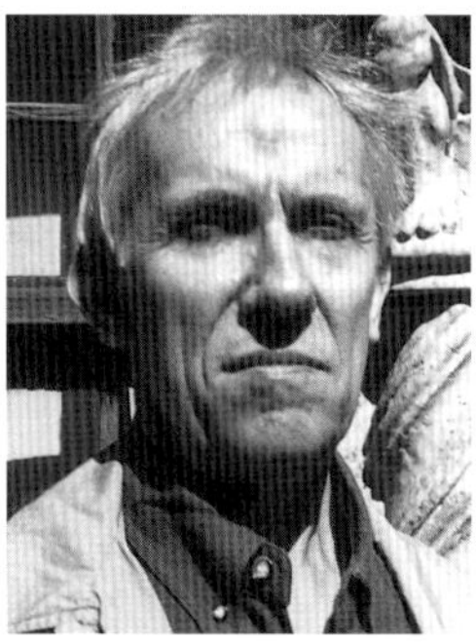

OLEG VASSILIEV

BORN Moscow 1931
EDUCATION Surikov Institute, Moscow
Currently lives in New York